Step By Step

Step By Step: A Comprehensive Guide

by Alex Genadinik

Step By Step: A Comprehensive Guide

Copyright © 2014 Alex Genadinik

All rights reserved.

ISBN:1495261840
ISBN-13: 978-1495261848

DEDICATION

Dedicated to my mother and grandmother who are the biggest entrepreneurs I know.

Step By Step: A Comprehensive Guide

CONTENTS

PART 1: GETTING BUSINESS IDEAS

i. How to get business ideas
ii. I have a great business idea but not sure what to do next
iii. How to tell if a business idea is good
iv. How to get feedback on your business ideas
v. Cheap market validation of your business ideas
vi. How to pitch your business ideas
vii. Why you should not ask others for business ideas

PART 2: BUSINESS THEORY AND FUNDAMENTALS

i. Types of business risk: product risk & market risk
ii. What to do if you have multiple ideas
iii. Business idea mistakes & bad business ideas
iv. Different types of business ideas, and which are best
v. Business idea evolution: how to make your business ideas better
vi. Top reasons businesses fail
vii. Home based business ideas or low risk business ideas
viii. Entrepreneur psychology
ix. Daydreaming about your business
x. Negative attitudes that can destroy a business
xi. Checklist to determine whether your business idea is good
xii. How to think about building your product

PART 3: PROTECTING YOUR INTELLECTUAL PROPERTY

i. 6 Ways to protect intellectual property

PART 4: PLANNING YOUR BUSINESS IDEA

i. Do you need to write a business plan?
ii. What is a business model?
iii. How to write a business plan for your business idea
iv. Examination on different revenue streams
v. How to maximize your revenue streams
vi. How to improve your sales funnel
vii. Financials: the cash flow statement
viii. Example of a popular business model: Freemium
ix. Identifying your target market

PART 5: BRINGING YOUR IDEA INTO REALITY

i. Should you register your business
ii. Difference between for profit business vs. non profit
iii. How to choose a great business name
iv. How to choose a great domain name for your website
v. How to find business partners or co-founders
vi. Customer development by Steve Blank
vii. The Lean Start-up by Eric Ries
viii. How to pursue your idea if you have a full time job & Should you quit your job if you have a business idea
ix. Starting a business with no business experience
x. The importance of getting a mentor & how to get a mentor to help you with your business idea
xi. When to hire a lawyer, accountant and get insurance
xii. How to fail fast and succeed faster
xiii. Skills you will need to make your business a

success
xiv. Some tips for early stage businesses
xv. Example of a timeline with steps for how to start your business

PART 6: RAISING MONEY

i. How much money should I raise to start a business
ii. Bootstrapping: how to start a business without money
iii. How to write a fundraising plan
iv. How to raise money for your business idea: 8 sources

PART 7: NEXT STEPS & RESOURCES

i. Further resources

FORWARD

The advice in this book is based on the experiences of the 300,000 entrepreneurs who have used my business apps to start a business, and the 1,000+ entrepreneurs whom I have helped personally.

Part 1: GETTING BUSINESS IDEAS

"Whether you think you can, or you think you can't, you are right."

- Henry Ford

i. How to get business ideas

Many people want to start a business, but do not know exactly where to start, or what might be a good business to get into. This guide on how to get business ideas is meant to help structure your thinking to help you get new business ideas, and increase the frequency with which you get business ideas.

Keep in mind, some business ideas may work for some individuals or founding teams, or at a certain points in time, but may not work for other people, or at other times. Success or failure depend on many factors. Some of those factors are the skills, strengths, motivations, ambitions and abilities of the entrepreneurs, in conjunction with overall timing, demographic trends, market conditions, and a number of other factors.

Before you decide on a single business idea which you will pursue with all your might, you want to get many business ideas of various quality as possible so that you have many to choose from. Later in this book, I'll explain how to determine which business ideas are the best for you, and how to improve the business ideas that you already have. For now, let's go over some fundamentals and patterns for how you can structure your thinking to increase the frequency with which you get business ideas.

First, Know Your Strengths And Weaknesses

It is a good strategy to first think about your personal and professional strengths. Your strengths can be professional skills and experience, industry connections, personal aptitudes, or even character traits that make you unique.

Are you an engineer who can build high quality, and complex technical products? Are you good at sales? Are you well-connected? Are you patient? Are you less patient than others? Are you a natural leader? Do you want to be a leader? Or do you maybe not want to be in the spotlight? Do you have a high moral and ethical I.Q? Whatever your strengths are, when you think about what kind of businesses are right for you, try to align the idea to take advantage of your strengths so that you can give your venture the most competitive edge. And don't be modest to yourself about your own strengths. It is important to acknowledge what your strengths are because starting a business is quite difficult. And you will need to make every little advantage work for you.

Some of the biggest strengths on which to focus are your field of education, professional experience, hobbies, and passions that you want to pursue moving forward.

Conversely, try to minimize your weaknesses. For example, if you are not technical, do not rush into businesses that require a lot of technical aptitude and skills. That does not mean you should be discouraged from those types of businesses. Many non-technical people have built successful technology companies in the past. It just means that you should think through it a bit more thoroughly because you will certainly need to have a solid strategy for how to get around whatever disadvantages you may have.

Additionally, many businesses require substantial upfront capital. If you are not wealthy, and are not able to raise high amounts of capital, business ideas that require substantial capital to get started may not be best for you because that capital requirement may become a barrier which will prevent you from ever being able to start your business.

The great news is that everyone has strengths. Even if your initial reaction is to feel that you don't have any real strengths, I bet you do. You just have to look inside yourself a little bit harder, and you will find many wonderful strengths. I promise. Everyone can find a niche in which they can give their business a competitive advantage. If you play to your strengths, you can give yourself a much higher chance to ultimately succeed. I am cheering for you!

What Are Your Interests and Passions?

If your business will be successful, you may end up working on this business for two, five, ten or maybe even more years. Think about what you want to do, and what would make you happy. Conversely, try not to get into business areas just for the money. If you start a business in an industry where you do not want to be, and money is the only motivation, or have no interest in, you may not find yourself being fulfilled. And if you lack real intrinsic motivation and excitement for the business idea, you may not find the inner strength to make it through the various business challenges and the difficult stages throughout the life of the business.

How Can You Improve the World?

This is very important. Having considered your passions and your strengths, keep in mind that your business is ultimately not completely for you. It is more for your customers. Perhaps your business is much more for your customers than it is for you because no matter how much you may love your business, if you have no customers, then ultimately you have no business.

Always think about your customers because without them no business can exist for long. Every business needs customers and your job is to find something you can do to make someone's life better, or improve something, or provide some value somewhere.

In fact, the old and traditional business school question that is the very first question typically used to evaluate a business idea is: "what problem does your business solve?" In fact, my website is named problemio.com precisely as a play on this traditional question of what problem the business solves.

That question is a bit narrow, of course. Not all businesses solve problems. Some businesses entertain, inform, teach, make something more efficient or easier to do, or benefit people in ways other than solving direct problems. Here are a few alternative, broader versions of that traditional question:

- How does your business help anyone or anything?
- Why should your business exist?
- What value does your business create?

So whoever you help, that person or business can become your customer. You can solve someone's problem, entertain them, teach them something, etc. You have to ultimately provide a great enough benefit to your customers. Keep in mind that the degree of how much help you are able going to be able to provide is directly proportional to how much you will be able to charge for the help you provide, and whether those customers would come back to buy from you again.

So as you go through your daily life, in the back of your mind, pay attention to everything that you see, use, hear others discussing, or come in contact with. If you notice some need, or something that can be improved, try to think of how to provide a solution to that need, and that will be the origin of your business ideas. Be vigilant of problems or imperfections of the world. Those are potential business opportunities if you can improve upon those things.

ii. I have a great business idea, but not sure what to do next

Very often, when people get business ideas, those ideas may seem original, unique, and exciting. But quite often, when business ideas come to us, those business ideas are in a random business space where we have little or no experience. That not only makes it difficult to determine whether this business idea is a good one, but it also makes the person who got that business idea not quite the right person to see this business idea through because they would have to learn everything about this new industry on the job. After all, beyond actually having this idea, what can this individual contribute to the business if they are not experienced in that field?

If you do not have any experience in the business area of the business idea, try to surround yourself with people who do have the appropriate experience and background. Those people can be either business partners, mentors or advisors. Typically, it takes 6-12 months for a founder to begin to fully understand the business space if they had no prior experience in that business space.

Additionally, start making contacts with people who are experienced in this space by simply attending some networking events, and chatting with people about your idea. You will have to do this as part of the process of getting feedback about your business idea, whether you have experience in this industry or not.

Create A Business Pitch

Before you begin talking to people about your business idea, I'd like to insert one step in the process. And that step is to come up with a business pitch which you can use when you do go out to get feedback. Once you have a clear business pitch, you will be able to explain your business idea very clearly. Otherwise, if you just had this idea a short time ago, it is probably very fresh and confused in your mind. And that might cause you to jumble up how you explain it to people, and confuse them. And confusing people is one of the worst things that can happen because the person from whom you are seeking feedback will not be able to really help if they don't understand your idea.

A full section on how to create a business pitch with a template and examples is found later in this book.

If you are wondering whether it is safe to tell your business idea to other people, and if you are concerned that they may steal the business idea that you share with them, there is a full section in this book dealing with issues around protecting your intellectual property. For now, I'll just leave you with the advice of only working with people whom you feel you can trust.

Get Feedback About Your Business Idea From Different People

As soon as you have a great business pitch, and can explain your business idea clearly, without worrying that other people may steal it (many people are concerned with this), it will be time to get feedback about your business idea from many different people. There are three types of people from whom you should get feedback on your business ideas: friends/family, professional peers, and domain experts.

You should certainly ask people whom you are close with like your friends and family. In fact, it is important to get the support of your family when you start a business. So try to get them involved in a supportive role. But don't just ask friends and family. Because your friends and family want the best for you, they will likely give you positive, subjective feedback. So try to get feedback from industry experts and people who can give you objective feedback. Much more is devoted to getting feedback from industry peers and domain experts in an upcoming section of this book.

Can You Create A Prototype?

If you still feel good about your business idea after discussing it with many different people, one of the next crucial steps will be to begin working on this business idea, and to create a prototype or an early version of the product that you envision.

While there are multiple guides on this later in the book on creating and launching a product, for now, as you examine a new business idea, just consider how difficult it might be for you to create the prototype for this business idea. Is it going to require a substantial amount of capital? Or can you build the prototype quickly and cheaply to test this idea in the market with real customers. Your goal will inevitably be to create the initial version of the product or service, and get an initial small group of people to use it. If you can do that relatively quickly and cheaply, that gives you a great advantage, and is a factor in determining if this particular business idea is the right one for you.

Keep in mind that not all businesses can create a prototype. If you are starting a restaurant, there is no prototype that you can make. But the advice of this section can still be used if you think about the potential barriers you might have for launching your business. Research the steps needed to get started on your particular business idea, and objectively evaluate how viable it might be to accomplish them. Often, the biggest barrier is having enough capital to get started.

iii. Further ways and strategies to tell if a business idea is good

People get business ideas all the time. But how does one decide which business ideas are good, and which are not worth pursuing? Here is a checklist with explanations for how to inform your thinking to determine whether a business idea is worth going after.

1) Do you have experience or expertise in the industry in which the business idea is in? If no, proceed with caution because it will be very difficult to determine whether various aspects of the idea will work out as you assume. Too many important details will be unknown, and that is quite dangerous.

2) Is the idea in a good market? A good market is one which is on the rise and expanding. While a bad market is one that is stagnant or is in a decline. For example, the mobile phone market is a good one because it is growing rapidly. But the print publishing market is not so good because it has been in a steady decline for a number of years. There is much more to understanding markets. In fact, whole books have been written on this. We will cover this topic more fully in an upcoming section of the book.

3) Does the idea go after a big enough market? Is the market for this idea in the billions of dollars, hundreds of millions, tens of millions, or less? If the market is too small, it will be difficult to make enough money to support a business. And if a market is too big, competition may be too fierce. Big markets are generally considered a good thing, but it is up to you to determine how competitive you can be with existing companies in that market, and what sweet spot market size is right for you.

4) Can you execute this idea? Many ideas out there are good. But you need to have the skills and ability to pull them off. For example, creating Google might be a good idea, but very few individuals in the world have the skills or resources to actually create such a company. Even a business as low-tech as a restaurant is very difficult to pull off. So you must make sure that you can actually execute the idea well.

5) Will this business have natural ways in which you will be able to promote it? Some businesses are easily discoverable, and are something people search for. Other types of businesses are often recommended to friends, and can spread through social invites and recommendations. But some types of businesses are not naturally discoverable or sharable. And that makes it very difficult to promote the

business once the business is operational. And that is a long-term dilemma for the founders of that business. Try to determine whether your business will be easy to market and promote, and whether there will be natural marketing strategies for it.

6) What demographic does the business idea target? Is the demographic lucrative? For example, if you make high-end jewelry, the demographic is lucrative because it targets wealthy people. But if you make something consumed by people who are below middle class in terms of financial status, then they may have a difficult time being able to afford your product if your product isn't a staple. And that will make it very difficult for you to get paying customers, and may force you to compete on price, which is a tricky and difficult strategy that is best to avoid if you can.

7) Will the business require more resources than you have? Resources are time, money, and skilled labor. Do you have a way to get all the resources you will need? Or would this business require more resources than you can realistically put together?

8) Is the business proven, or something new and innovative? If the business is something that has been done before with success (think cleaners, dentists, home repair, etc), then it is considered to be proven. But if it is something innovative (for example, unique types of websites), that can be very good, but the burden of proof for whether this business should exist is up to you. That means extra risk that accompanies the extra potential reward.

9) Are there competitors in the space in which the idea is in? How well would you be able to compete with them? Are they strong? Or are they weak? Be careful not to compete against loved and strong companies. That is the most difficult kind of

company to beat. Also be careful of markets where there are no competitors at all. That could be a red flag that this market is not as great as you might think. One of the best situations is where there is a large market where the incumbent companies are not very liked. If you can come in, and create something better, you can easily take their customers away.

10) Is this business idea something you want to be doing for a few years? If you are successful, you will be a part of this business for a long time. Is that something you actually want to do? That is worth considering.

11) Is the market you are in heavily regulated? If so, you may have legal challenges that will slow the business down, and increase the risk and costs of starting it.

12) Does the business idea solve a real need or make someone's life materially better or easier? Or does the business provide some great value somehow? If so, then there will likely be demand for the business. But if not, you may have a difficult time generating demand.

13) Has this idea been tried before? If this idea has been tried by many companies which have all failed, you must research why that happened, and make sure that you do not repeat the same mistakes that those companies did. If many of those companies succeeded, you must figure out how to differentiate from them to be unique enough, yet still be successful.

iv. How to get feedback on your business ideas

We all know that we need to get feedback when we are trying to figure out whether our business ideas are good or not. But many of us make the same, very common mistakes when it comes to getting feedback about a business idea. In this section, we will explore some common mistakes people make when trying to get feedback about their business ideas. We will also go over some things you can do which will help you in the process of getting feedback.

Common Mistakes When Getting Feedback On Business Ideas

The most common mistake people make is that they don't actually get enough feedback. I realize that sounds basic, but that truly is the biggest mistake. Most people realize this mistake as they are making it, but just about everyone makes this mistake anyway. A part of the problem is that people are very private about their business ideas and want to protect those ideas, which makes sharing the idea difficult. Another contributing factor to this issue is that people rush to start without spending enough time planning the business. Lastly, a large contributing factor to this mistake is that there just aren't that many domain experts that are ready to spend time with entrepreneurs to provide feedback. Domain experts and industry professionals are usually busy and are difficult to get a hold of. That makes it difficult to get feedback from many of them.

Even if you are not protective about your business idea, getting feedback requires quite a bit of work. You have to do lots of outreach to people, then meet with them, and take time to think about the opinions they offer. The entire process can take weeks if not months in order to get a good amount of feedback. What happens most of the time is that people just get a few pieces of feedback or advice, and stop there.

Usually, the first people you talk to will be people whom you know, and most likely they will sugarcoat the feedback. But because you may want to believe the positive feedback, you may take that as objective truth, and believe the overly positive feedback and stop there. But that would be a mistake because that feedback was nowhere near in quality and objectivity of where it needed to be.

Another mistake people make is that they get feedback almost exclusively from friends and family because those are the people who are easy to reach. Of course, savvy industry experts are busy, and you probably do not know them personally. So the majority of options most of us have at our disposal is to ask our friends and family. But our friends and family will give either subjectively positive feedback, or feedback that is very protective of us, or just isn't savvy enough. So our job as entrepreneurs is to do what we can to get objective feedback from real industry experts.

As you are getting feedback, just talking to people is not enough because the entire conversation is very theoretical and the potential results of it are limited. If it is simple or cheap for you to create a prototype of your product, try to create that prototype first, so that when you do get feedback, the feedback can be about that real physical prototype and not just a theoretical concept.

Dealing With Negative Feedback

Sometimes you will get negative feedback, and sometimes you will get extremely negative feedback that may partially border on insulting you and your business. It does happen. If you discuss your business with enough people, statistically, this is inevitable.

Extremely negative feedback can be quite shocking. The most important thing is not to get angry, or insulted by it. Take a deep breath and step back. Always be polite and try to understand what exactly is causing such vitriol for that person. Maybe they are just having a bad day, or maybe they didn't quite understand some of the nuances your business idea.

If the person remains angry give them some space, and approach them in a few days in order to give them a chance to get over their anger. That may help to have a calmer conversation, and you will have a chance to turn that person into a fan by showing that you really do care. But it may be an equally good idea to leave that person alone altogether because you do not want that kind of extreme and unnecessary negativity around you or your business.

If you can get past the negativity, sometimes you might discover that people who are very negative about your business bring up points that are valid. Maybe they overemphasize their points, but nevertheless, they may have some valid points. All feedback should be considered and thought about.

Further in the book, we'll cover various psychological aspects of being an entrepreneur, and take a look at this issue a bit more closely.

Experts Don't Always Know

Additionally, if you do get to talk to experts in your field, and they give you negative feedback about your idea, while that may be something to certainly think about, their word isn't the final word. Certainly think about what they have to say, but keep in mind that it is up to you to make this business idea happen. If you believe in it, you can try to prove them wrong. History is littered with cases where experts have said that something can't work, and then that thing worked. Just don't disregard people's feedback. Always think about it and give it full consideration. Every opinion can be learned from. What you ultimately do is, of course, up to you. But make sure you have thought through every point of feedback so that you have the most holistic view of the situation from which to then make your decisions.

How To Get The Advice Of Experts

It is very difficult to get meetings with real experts because they are usually very busy, and they have multiple people just like you who regularly ask them for help. Some things you can try in order to get experts to give you their time are:

- Ask to meet for only 5 minutes or less.
- Ask to meet them wherever they are, at any time that is convenient for them.
- Ask your question in the initial email. If it is interesting for them, and simple to answer, they may just answer it right there and then.
- Use your connections on LinkedIn to see who can recommend you to them. A solid recommendation can go a long way to getting you a meeting.
- Reach out to them on social media and begin building a relationship there.
- Offer to help them with something they are working on first instead of immediately asking for a favor.

v. Cheap market validation for your business ideas

Not doing market research and validation is a common and

very costly mistake that entrepreneurs make far too often when evaluating new business ideas. It is an unforced error of sorts, which can easily be avoided.

In the midst of overall excitement about starting their venture, many people neglect to test the idea in real-world scenarios. Instead, with all their will and optimism, they dive right into building their company.

As a very prudent step, entrepreneurs are encouraged to test their ideas on a small scale in the real world, and observe how well their ideas/products/services are received by their targeted consumers.

In addition to learning how viable your overall idea really is, there are many additional benefits of doing this. You can cheaply discover early glitches in your process, areas where your quality could be better, and where you are not meeting the needs of your consumers. This is actually something you would be doing if you were running the company on a larger scale as well. The only difference is that it is far cheaper to get the kinks out of your business early than fixing them later.

Keep in mind, not every type of business or product can be tested or market-validated equally well. Sometimes you have to get creative in how you validate your business idea in the market.

Examples Of Market Validation

If you are thinking of opening a restaurant or have a new and unique food item, why not experiment with a food truck or a food cart? Food trucks can also be very expensive but you can either lease one, or try to have your products sold from an existing one to see whether people like or dislike your menu. And the cost of a food truck is still orders of magnitude cheaper than starting a restaurant.

If you have a clothing or fashion item that you design and want to sell, do not print large numbers of them right away. Have a relatively small batch made, and try to see how well the products would sell at local fashion events or fairs. That will help you see how potential customers react to the clothing you made when they see it, and try it on. It will also give you a chance to talk to them to see how your products could be better, and why they do or do not like your products. Plus the sales metrics that you would get from doing this would give you a better sense for whether the risk of printing/creating many such items is a good risk to take. Also, you can approach various smaller fashion stores with samples of the clothing you made to see whether they would carry your items. The feedback from them would also help to get a sense of how people who are savvy in your fashion space perceive the products.

If your business is a new type of a website, look at other similar websites, and possibly contact the people who run those sites. They may turn out to be kind enough to share what the difficulties of that space are. Or if your idea is complex, and would cost tens of thousands of dollars to build, consider simplifying it by taking out a number of features. That would make it possible to launch a very lite version of the planned website, and add additional features one by one as the website grows. We will cover this in more depth later in this book when we discuss the Lean Start-up methodology from Eric Ries.

If you have a business that requires sales, and want to know how much demand you will have once you invest into launching the company, one interesting but slightly controversial approach may be to start selling before you can actually perform the services, or send products.

This will give you a sense of how much sales you will be able to generate without having to buy inventory or hire staff. And if people do want to buy whatever products or services you are selling, just tell these customers that you will put them on a waiting list for when you are able to fill their order, and that you are working on fulfilling their order ASAP.

You can also simply tell them you cannot provide what you were selling, and give them a full refund. That will let you test whether you will be able to generate sales, and help you determine whether you should hire staff or buy up inventory.

Whatever your business is, just be creative and make sure you get real-world market data. It will help you to have a deeper understanding of the overall business environment for your idea, and the viability of your idea in the market. It will also help you find flaws in your business idea cheaply so that the overall plan of action can be refined and perfected in a less expensive way.

vi. How to pitch your business ideas

When you talk about your company or pitch your business, you want to be brief and extremely clear. This helps people quickly understand your business, and ask further questions if they are interested.

Here is a template for how you can explain your company very clearly at a high level in about 30 seconds. There are 3 to 5 main points you need to cover based on how much you want to divulge.

Business Idea Pitch Template

1) My name is (your name here). I am (planning/started/growing) company (fill in your company name)
2) Which is a (website? physical store? mobile app? restaurant? service?)
3) For (fill in your target audience here).
4) The company aims to (fill in what is the purpose of the company, or what does it do for the target audience)
5) By (explain what the company will do differently or uniquely)

This template comes from Adeo Ressi who is the founder of the Founders Institute.

Business Idea Pitch Examples

Here are a couple of examples of business pitches using this template.

Example for a restaurant: I am opening a high end Italian restaurant in downtown London because there are currently no such restaurants there.

Example for a website: I recently launched a website for people who like to work on classic cars. The website has articles and videos with tutorials for how to work on cars.

Example for a gardening company: I am in the planning stages of opening a residential lawn care and gardening company in San Francisco which will focus on providing the best customer experience with the lowest prices.

Example for a technology: I am in the planning stages of a mobile app company in New York. The company will create mobile apps that help people create business plans on their mobile devices.

Purpose Of The Business Pitch

The most important thing your pitch needs to accomplish is to be clear. If it is not clear, and the person listening to the pitch does not understand it, then the whole point of pitching the business is lost. That makes clarity the number one priority. That is why the pitch examples are so short and to the point. Once you become good at explaining your business clearly with short pitches like that, you can add various components to your business pitch such as how you will make money, the competition, and more about the product and the secret sauce.

But remember, as you add various components to your pitch, the level of clarity must remain very high. Also, once you become more comfortable with pitching the business, you can try to add humor, or make the pitch personalized to the listener, or be inspirational in some way.

Longer Business Pitches

If your initial pitch goes well, you may engage in further conversation with whoever you are pitching. If they are an investor, they might invite you to give them a longer pitch of about 5-10 minutes and ask for a business plan or a slide deck presentation.

Giving Your Business Pitch At Event Presentations

As your business grows, you may get the opportunity to present your business at events. The typical time a business gets to present at an event is about 3-5 minutes. In these 3-5 minutes, you must go over the basics as you would in your 1-

minute pitch, but add more depth about the product, have a prepared demo, explain your secret sauce, and possibly your competitive environment and what makes your business different.

Show Your Product In Addition To The Pitch

If you are presenting your business at an event or during a second meeting with someone, it is much more powerful if you can show something rather than just telling people about it. For that reason, it is good to have a website or a prototype that you can show along with your presentation.

Note: if you are just pitching someone during your first meeting with them, do not show a prototype or your website unless they specifically ask you to. In that case, showing your website or prototype is considered bad practice.

vii. Why you should not ask people for new business ideas

Over time, hundreds of people have written to me, asking me for business ideas. Unfortunately, I always have to give everyone the same answer which is that I can't give everyone a business idea because I would give everyone the same business idea, and as we already covered, a business idea must be a match for the abilities, strengths, and passions of the entrepreneur who will be running that business.

Additionally, all business ideas have strengths and weaknesses. Some of my favorite ideas do not make much money, but have a heavier than usual focus on leaving a positive influence on the world. That makes these ideas more risky as businesses because their focus is less on making money, but more on interesting as benevolent projects. So when choosing an idea to pursue, the goals of the entrepreneurs have to be taken into account, and my goals are different from the goals of many other people who ask me for business ideas.

The right thing to do isn't to ask others for business ideas, but rather to start working on something that you are interested in, and ask for an opinion on how to improve the business idea that you may currently have. We will have much more on this in the chapter of this book that focuses on starting the actual business.

Part 2: Understanding business theory and fundamentals

i. 3 Types of business risk: financial risk, market risk and product risk

There are three types of risk you should think about when evaluating a business idea. The first type of risk is obvious. It is simply financial risk that you are willing to take. The other two types of risk have more to do with actually building and growing the business. They are the product risk and market risk. Let's take a closer look at all three.

Financial Risk

Every business has some degree of financial risk. But that risk varies. A web business can have financial risk as low as a few hundred dollars if you can build the website on your own. And a restaurant can have financial risk of up to hundreds of thousands of dollars.

It is up to you to determine how much financial risk you are willing to take, and what your limit is. When you evaluate business ideas, try to determine whether they fit into the financial risk that you have determined that is acceptable for you.

Market Risk

Market risk is the general risk that the market in which you are planning to do business will not accept your product or service, and that there will be no traction for your product. Every business has some degree of market risk. To put it simply, the market risk is that your target customers will not buy the product for one reason or another.

Parts of the risk are that you may not be able to out-market your competition, or that the customers you are going after may not really like or buy the product or service that you will be selling. This is a very real risk because there are so many products and services that consumers are able to choose from that they tend to have a strong indifference towards new products. That means that your product must really delight them in one way or another because if you can't get market adoption and generate sales, that will be a serious obstacle for the survivability of the business.

This is why we do all the market and idea validation before starting the business. It is to minimize market risk.

Product Risk

Product risk is the risk that you may not actually be able to bring the product to market within the resources (time, money) that you have available to you. And if you do deliver the product, the risk is also that the product may not work exactly as well as hoped, promised or envisioned. Every business has a degree of product risk, but just like financial risk, product risk can be mitigated and kept low.

For example, if you are building a very basic website like a blog, the product risk is very low. You can launch this product within a day. But if you are building a complex website that would take months of engineering time to complete, then the product risk is quite high because there are many things that can happen before the product can be launched. You may run out of money, the engineers might quit, some technical challenges may be greater than initially assumed, etc. And all that adds to the risk that the product may never be launched, or that it isn't up to par even if it does get launched.

To decrease product risk, you can start with a more basic version of your site, and improve it iteratively, feature by feature. That will give you the flexibility you need to change direction or make any adjustments to the product.

ii. What to do if you have more than one business idea

Having multiple business ideas is a very common situation that many new and experienced entrepreneurs often face. It is a natural occurrence because entrepreneurs tend to be ambitious people who want to do many things. The trick, of course, is to know how to handle this situation correctly.

You Must Choose Just One Idea Out of Many

The truth is, that in almost all cases, to make your business a success, you have to choose only one idea, and put all your effort into it. You will find that even if you put all your effort into a single business idea, it will still be very difficult to turn that idea into a successful business. So the more you can focus on the single idea, the greater your chances of success will be.

How To Choose Which Idea To Go After

There are a number of criteria that can help you choose which idea is the best to go after. One of the most important criteria is your natural instinct (sometimes referred to as your gut reaction). First, ask yourself which of your ideas do you feel would be better and what feels right to you.

Which Of The Ideas Are You Most Passionate About?

Being passionate, or very interested in a particular field can give you a very big advantage when you are pursuing your business idea. Being interested in the subject matter will keep you moving forward through the difficult times, and will help you persevere through the many business challenges you will face along the way. It will also enable you to represent your company in a more natural and genuine way because you will be more at home in that environment.

Which of The Ideas Can You Actually Do Well?

Another practical point to consider is which of the business ideas you can successfully pursue. For example, if one of your ideas requires $100,000 to start, and the other idea requires $5,000 and you have never raised money before, the $5,000 idea may seem more attractive because it is more feasible and more practical.

Similarly, if you are not experienced with technology, but one of the ideas requires proficiency in technology, that may be a yellow flag that this is possibly not the right business idea for you unless you can partner with someone who is proficient in technology.

Which Idea Takes Advantage Of Your Strengths?

If you have professional experience in a particular field, pursuing a business in that field can give you a number of advantages because you can leverage the knowledge, connections, and experience that you have gathered over the years of working in that area.

The opposite of that would be pursuing a business in an area in which you have little or no experience. If you do that, the first 6-12 months will be largely very expensive learning on your part. And that is something to consider avoiding.

Proper Planning Can Help Avoid Many Mistakes

If you do not have much experience in the field of one of your ideas, it is a good idea to slow down and do some proper planning and research. Finding potential problems and pitfalls during the planning stage is much cheaper than to run into those pitfalls when you are going full speed and executing your business. The things to plan for are the monetization strategy, understanding of expenses, and understanding of how to build a competitive product within your business niche. Also, it takes time to get to understand the precise needs of your target consumers and their consumption patterns. And last but not least is your marketing plan. You must have a great plan for how you will effectively market to your target consumers and get clients.

We will focus more deeply on business planning later in the book. For now, just use these criteria to narrow your multiple business ideas down to your favorite idea. Additionally, we will cover some of the common business idea mistakes in an upcoming section of this book. You may notice a mistake that you may be about to make, which can also influence which business idea you ultimately choose to go with.

iii. Are there such things as bad business ideas

If you think about it, some very unusual business ideas have worked out very well in the past. Conversely, there are many very common business ideas that ultimately do not work. There are many factors that can influence the outcome of a business. Some of these reasons are the overall strategy, positioning, marketing, how hard the entrepreneurs starting those companies were willing to work, their perseverance, global demographic trends, availability of resources, timing, product quality, market and economic conditions, and many other factors.

As an example, consider a very common type of business: a restaurant. Many restaurants have been successful in the past while many have also failed. For a restaurant to be successful, there are many things that have to go right, starting from the planning stage. For example, if the restaurant is in an area where there are not many people passing by, it will be difficult and more costly to acquire new customers. If the food is not great or too expensive for its quality, the restaurant will not have many repeat customers and get bad online reviews, which will make it even more difficult and expensive to acquire new customers. There are many things that can go wrong. The staff may be unfriendly. The economy might be weak. A better restaurant can open up next door. The business can run out of money before it breaks even. Or the founder just did not have enough knowledge or experience in the industry which led to too many mistakes.

As you can see, in one instance a business idea can be good, and in another situation, the same idea might be bad. Think about Twitter.com as an example. Today it is a multi-billion dollar business. But when that company was young, few people understood it, and labeled it as a terrible business idea. So you really never know.

Mismatch Of Business To Founding Team

Different people have different strengths. The founder does not have to possess all the core skills that the business requires. But together, the nucleus of the founding team really should possess the core skills required by the type of business that they are starting.

For example, Internet/tech businesses typically require the founding teams to have a tech background. Food-related businesses require culinary or hospitality industry background. Product-centric companies require ability to make great products and sell them. Some businesses need to raise a lot of money while others need to get a lot of publicity. The founding team must have the skills for whatever the business will require. And if the founding team does not have the necessary skills to successfully start and grow that business, that particular business idea may not be a great fit for them, making it bad for them even if the idea itself isn't ultimately a bad one.

Lack of Experience In A Field Requires Approximately 6-12 Months Of Learning The Industry

If the founding team does not have strong experience in the industry in which the business idea is in, that will necessitate a lot of learning on the job, which will in turn cause many errors and steps in unsure directions. Small errors are not difficult to recover from, but gross mistakes can be very costly in terms of time and money. Before having to pay for these mistakes out of the bank account of your own business, it may be better to do some work in this area as an employee, or maybe start with a smaller project just to learn the ropes cheaply.

A very common mistake people make is that they try to quickly go big with a business area which is in a business niche in which they do not have enough experience. Trying to go big quickly, sounds great in theory, but it can be very damaging to the business if it doesn't happen the right way. The bigger you try to go, the bigger and more costly the mistakes will be as well.

Lack of Circumstance-Idea Match

Sometimes the business idea is just too dependent on the overall market and other outside conditions. If those conditions are not favorable to the business, it can be time to reconsider the business idea. Of course, conversely, most business types are cyclical (that means their success correlates with timing of the overall economy which tends to go through good and bad multi-year cycles).

Think about how the trends in global and local economies will affect your business. Not taking that into consideration can leave you with significant risk.

iv. Top-10 business idea mistakes

Now let's go over the top-10 business idea mistakes which can significantly damage your business.

1) Not Understanding The Financials Of The Business

Yes, I know, finances are boring and often intimidating. But I strongly suggest to focus on the financials of your business, and understand them very deeply. Not having a strong sense of costs, revenue, profit margins, and overall market size is one of the biggest mistakes that can be made. But don't worry, we will focus on this further in the book.

2) Not Having A Solid Understanding Of Target Customer Demographics

Very often, when asked who their target customers are, new and eager entrepreneurs say "everyone." But it is nearly impossible for a young business to create a product that pleases "everyone." Additionally, it is also very difficult to market to everyone because in reality, most people are indifferent to various products and your marketing efforts will be largely wasted. What you need to do is market to people who will be excited about your product. And you must identify who that group of people might be.

Savvy entrepreneurs know to have a strong focus on their target market. If asked, they can usually discuss the age, affluence level, education level, lifestyle, behavior patterns, and consumption patterns of their target customers. Knowing all this about their customers helps them create products that delight that group of people. Plus it is much easier to come up with a marketing plan since there is a strong focus.

We will focus more on understanding your target market in an upcoming section of this book.

3) Misunderstanding Of The Risk

Quite often, people go into business because they have no other choice. Sometimes it is due to a difficult economy and the inability to find work. Sometimes it is because of an unavoidable career change. Whatever the reason may be, quite often people see the business as a way to make money and pull themselves out of the financial difficulties they may be in.

Unfortunately, statistics show that most businesses fail. The failure rate of businesses started by first-time entrepreneurs is extremely high. Even the businesses which do not fail, take some time to make a profit and may even cost you money.

Furthermore, a business requires quite a bit of your time, adds stress that may put a strain on your family and social situations, which may in turn, cause more financial stress. So at first, a business is something you give a lot to; not the other way around.

4) Not Understanding The Type Of Business Idea You Have

Business ideas are not created equal. I tend to split them into two types of ideas: innovative and commoditized (more on this distinction later in the book). A commoditized business is something that has been done many times before. Some examples are restaurants, home repair, lawn care business, dentist offices, etc. And innovative businesses are usually new types of technology-enabled businesses such as new website ideas, new app ideas, and new gadgets.

The core difference is that if you are starting a commoditized business, there is nothing about that business you should not know before you start. It has been done so many times before that you can find the right mentors and information, and get to understand most of the necessary nuances about this business before you start. On the other hand, with innovative businesses, it is often very difficult to know what that business will eventually become. Typically, in an innovative business, what you start with, is not what you end up with because you have to keep constantly experimenting, and refining your strategy.

5) Worrying That The Idea Will Be Stolen

If your idea is innovative and has not been tried before, it can be scary to share the idea with others for fear that they may copy it. No one should tell you whether you should or should not protect your ideas. That is your decision since it is your business. But here are some things to consider when deciding whether you will be open or private about the idea you are working on.

Since an idea needs to constantly change and evolve, one of the ways you get direction for how to evolve the idea is by listening to the opinions and feedback from others. You do not have to take everyone's advice, but you should definitely give it a fair amount of thought. Eventually this process will give you further ideas for how to make your original idea even better.

By being too private with their business ideas, many people limit the amount of feedback they can get. That often limits the potential for how that idea can improve and evolve.

Plus the only advantage you get by being private about your idea is that no one will steal your idea prior to you launching the product. But once your product is live, it is in public view which means that anyone can copy your ideas once your product is live.

6) Choosing The Wrong Or Unproven Team

Your team must be made up of people who do amazing work, share the same vision, and very importantly, have worked together before. Paul Graham, founder of Y-Combinator, which is the top start-up incubator in the world, constantly talks about how in his incubator, teams which have worked on projects before, have had a much higher success rate than teams who have not worked together before.

Additionally, make sure that your team possesses all the skill sets you will need to start and grow this business, and that everyone does top-quality work. Team member skill sets should not overlap too much, but rather be complementary to each other. And lastly, make sure you work with good people whom you can trust and who you like. If the business is successful (I sincerely hope it will be), you will need to spend a very long time working with your team members. Conversely, getting the wrong founders out of a project can be a costly and poisonous process that you want to avoid.

7) Not Having A Solid Understanding Of Market Size

Market size discussion can get complex. For now, let's keep it very simple. There are 3 market sizes: small, medium, and big. A small market is approximately under 10 million dollars. That may seem big, but that is tiny for a market. Medium size markets can range from 10 million to 200 million as a rough estimate. Again, this may seem large, but you can not make a billion dollar company in a 200 million dollar market. To make a very big company, you must be in a very big market, hopefully a multi-billion dollar market.

Knowing your market size can help you determine how much money you can realistically make with the current incarnation of your business idea. Also, you can get a sense of the types of challenges you will face. If your market is big, you will face enormous competition. If your market is small, the problem might be that there may be too little revenue potential. And if the market is mid-size, then you may or may not face the issues I just mentioned depending on other nuances of that market.

So try to make sure you have a sense for the market size you are after. This will influence a large part of the strategy for everything else.

8) Not Having A Solid Understanding Of Market History

Knowing the history of the market you are going after is just as important as knowing your market size. Very likely, there have been many companies with identical or very similar ideas as yours. You must understand why the companies who came before you succeeded or failed. Learning those lessons will help you understand how to steer your business, and what pitfalls to avoid. As often happens in life, it is much better to learn from the mistakes and successes of others than from your own mistakes.

9) Not Understanding How To Market And Promote The Business

Marketing and promoting your business is really the lifeline of your business. If you can get new customers, great. If you cannot, then there is no business.

Many people go into a business without a good understanding of how to promote their business. Too often, people go into a business with their marketing strategy being to hand out business cards, post about their business on Facebook or Twitter, and hand out flyers. While those strategies are fine, and may work for a few businesses, they are often not nearly enough of a marketing strategy because they do not scale, and often do not reach most of the target consumers.

So try to have a very strong marketing strategy planned

before you dive into a particular business idea.

10) Thinking As A Marketer And Neglecting Great Customer Experience

Just about every business owner wants to grow their business, get as many customers as possible, and make as much money from those customers as possible. That creates a natural tendency to focus on selling as much as possible and maximizing profit as much as possible. This a very common experience for business owners. But keep in mind that your product quality is incredibly important. So make sure you are not just putting all your focus on how to sell your product, and that you are devoting enough time and resources to constantly improving the quality of your product or service. Make sure your customers are delighted by your product or service, and feel like they are getting a great value. Chances are that this strategy will pay off in the short and long term because if your customers love your product, they will do some of the marketing for you by recommending it to friends, leaving positive testimonials, and helping in a variety of other ways.

v. Different categories of business ideas

There are many ways to categorize different business ideas. For our purposes, let's categorize them into three general types: innovative, commoditized, and hybrid which is a mix of the two. Let's examine each.

Innovative Business Ideas

These are ideas for new kinds of websites, mobile apps,

gadgets, smart phones, tablets, or other electronic devices.

The great thing about these kinds of ideas is that they lead the way for everyone else. They create whole new markets and for a short time, get a lead over other kinds of businesses. They tend to also have potential to grow rapidly, and for that reason, are attractive investments for venture capital and seed investors.

The problem with innovative businesses is that precisely because they are new, no one really knows how great or small the demand for them will be, and how well they will ultimately grow, or whether they will find market acceptance.

Figuring out how to get the market to accept their products, and how to market and grow their business is up to the founders of companies with innovative products. So while innovating is exciting, it adds a whole layer of risk (remember market risk?) which is that the customers may not ultimately be interested in those particular innovative products. More traditional companies never have to face this particular risk. Let's consider some types of business ideas that do not have that kind of a market adoption risk.

Commoditized Business Ideas

There are many types of businesses which have been around for a long time that do not have to innovate, and can still be great businesses. Just think about the different businesses in any city. Every city needs restaurants, cleaners, dentists, mechanics, people to fix homes, etc. The list goes on. The core differences between these types of businesses and innovative businesses are that these tend to be service-based business with a local focus. For that reason these have less potential to become multi-billion dollar businesses, and typically do not grow beyond the local area.

Additionally, they do not grow as quickly.

But the great thing is that there is no risk of demand. There is definitely demand for these kinds of businesses as long as the entrepreneur can provide the service with a high-enough degree of quality, and the economy doesn't completely crater.

IMPORTANT NOTE: If you are considering starting what we call here a commoditized business, since it is a commoditized, and has been done successfully many times in the past, there should be almost no part of starting or growing this business that you are not sure of once you start. There is knowledge out there for how to start it, promote it, run it, how much money is needed to start it, and how to spend that money wisely. Your challenge is to find and learn this information. Having mentors who have created such a business before is a great option if you can get it. So try to get mentors who have successfully started such businesses in the past. A great mentor can steer you away from many potential mistakes, and help you succeed.

Hybrid Business Ideas

Hybrid business ideas are the kinds of ideas which borrow a little bit from both, the commoditized ideas and innovative ideas. Here are some examples.

- Restaurants that serve fusion cuisine. They are restaurants which are traditional types of businesses, but they innovate with their menu.

- Websites to find school tutors. These kinds of sites take a local service that has been around for a long time, and make it easier to find tutors.

vi. Business idea evolution: how to make your business idea better

In this section we'll examine how business ideas change and evolve over time, and how you can make your business ideas better.

Business Ideas Should Not Be Static Nor Allowed To Just Sit There

Imagine if the person who first invented the wheel would not have actually created the wheel after getting the idea for it. Well, just as the saying goes, someone would have re-created the wheel shortly after. However, as imperfect as analogies can sometimes be, the point illustrated here is that if an idea is not worked on, and is allowed to just sit there, someone else will come along and take it from theory (just an idea) to reality (creating the actual wheel).

Try to test your ideas and act on them if you can. Taking ideas from theory to reality is a creative process. Chances are that the idea is in some way imperfect. That is OK. By taking the steps to take the idea from theory to reality you will find where the idea may be lacking, and improve those aspects of the initial business idea. In fact, it is expected that your idea would initially be imperfect. In fact, success at first try should be highly surprising. So you must put your imperfect idea in motion, and evolve it to become better and better by consistently improving it and working at it. The great thing about trying ideas out is that no matter the outcome, there is some learning that happens along the way, and that learning gives rise to new ideas that are better.

Moving The Business Idea Forward And Evolving It

As the entrepreneur keeps testing out his or her ideas, the original idea begins to change and evolve, and becomes better. Keep in mind that the evolution is not a linear improvement. Instead, it is a mixture of some steps forward and some steps back. Although there have been many cases where some great idea just came to someone, most world innovation was a result of continuous trial and error and persistent work rather than a single light bulb moment.

As the entrepreneur keeps learning about what was not quite right with the original version of his or her idea, he or she continuously gets slightly better ideas which then become the main idea that is being brought into reality out of theory. The same cycle repeats as the entrepreneur tries that new idea out, and again learns about which parts of that idea were not quite right and what worked well. As the entrepreneur works to refine that new idea, they come up with ways to make it even better. Over time, by virtue of working on the original idea, the original idea evolves quite tremendously. But the idea only evolves if it is being worked on very intensely. Hard work is key here.

As the entrepreneur keeps trying, the original idea continuously evolves, moves forward, and becomes less and less recognizable. Anyone doubting this should search in Google for "First Yahoo homepage 1994." to see an example of how Yahoo evolved over time from where they started.

This may be partially ironic to anyone who has ever tried to protect their business idea because if anyone tried to steal or copy that first idea, they would have gotten a really bad idea while the entrepreneur who continuously worked on the idea would have probably evolved that idea into something more worthwhile over time.

Case Study Example

That brings us to the case study from my own experience as an entrepreneur that I want to share as a great example of how business ideas evolve. I will share how my original idea for my current Problemio.com business apps evolved from its first day in 2012 to its present state in early 2014.

My original idea for this business was not to make mobile apps at all. Originally I wanted to make a public online forum for people to brainstorm and discuss solutions to various problems in the world. Some problems would be solved by creating businesses to solve them. So essentially, the community would create the plan for a business to solve a particular problem, and someone from the community would try that out as a business. You see how different my idea was in the beginning? Everything about it changed except for the main goal of helping entrepreneurs.

When I first started on this idea, since I was not sure whether this original idea of mine was any good, I asked many people whom I knew about what they thought of this idea. Half of them liked the idea and half of them did not quite understand it. So I built that website because it was simple for me to build it. And having a live website would help me see whether people would want to use something like this. To my disappointment, no one really wanted to use it. So I started to change the site. Over time, I changed it many times in an attempt to make the original idea work, each time learning more and more.

I learned many things along the way. One of the things I learned was that people did not want to openly discuss their business ideas, but instead they wanted private business planning tools and private help to plan their own business. And people really needed guidance in planning their business because most people were first-time entrepreneurs.

I also found that it was much easier for me to market this tool as a mobile app than a website, so eventually I built a mobile app on the Android platform to allow people to plan a business right on the app.

That app was much more successful than the original website idea, and users liked it quite a bit. But many people using the app constantly kept contacting me and asking for business ideas, how they can raise money for their business, and how they can grow their business.

I kept answering those questions, but since so many of those questions were about the same topic, that led me to the next idea which was to create apps covering those topics as well. So I created the 4-app course for starting a business covering business ideas, business planning, marketing and fundraising. And that is how I got a failed website to become a successful mobile app series. But the business idea evolution doesn't stop there. After about 200,000 downloads of my apps, I started my own YouTube channel covering those same 4 topics. That channel now has over 400 business tutorials (www.youtube.com/user/Okudjavavich) and I release a new tutorial daily. As the apps grew, I also started a podcast on the same topics, and then wrote two books on the same topic as well. This book is the first of the two. The second book covers how to grow your business after you actually start it. I could have never imagined that creating a business idea website in 2012 would lead me to write two books in 2014. That journey was only made possible by continuously trying different strategies, learning, and evolving whatever the current state of my ideas was at any particular time.

vii. Top reasons businesses fail

At one point I surveyed over 1,000 people who were using my apps, asking them what happened with their business, whether they failed or succeeded, and what were their biggest challenges.

The biggest challenges people generally face are: not having the right experience, not having enough (or any) money, and choosing business ideas that they probably cannot pursue successfully.

To elaborate on the last point. To be able to pursue a business idea well, the founding team must have experience and resources needed to compete within the market in which the business idea is in. For example, if a business sells shoes online, they have to compete with some of the biggest websites in the world like shopping.com or amazon.com, zappos.com, and many other established online retailers. To truly compete with them, you have to out-compete them on marketing, pricing and other issues. Since they have been building a brand for the last 15 years, it is nearly impossible to out-market them because Amazon is nearly synonymous with online shopping these days. And it is even more difficult to out-compete them on price in any sustainable way because they have been improving logistics to decrease prices for the past 15 years. A huge part of the defensibility of their business is that they are able to out-compete other companies on price.

Here is a further breakdown of the biggest types of challenges new businesses tend to face. My study was not scientific, so here are some rough percentages of what most people reported to be challenges for them.

Note: a single business typically reported multiple of the challenges noted below the same time:

90% of the people noted lack of funding to be a problem
75% of the people noted insufficient marketing and inability to get clients to be a big problem
70% of the people admitted that they didn't realize the amount of work that would be necessary
30% of the people were stuck planning their business and could not move past the planning phase
20% of the people admitted that they realized that their business idea was just bad and quit early
60% of the people had a difficult time getting past the legal issues needed to start a business
40% of the people admitted that their team wasn't good enough to start this business

So when you are planning the strategy for your business idea, try to plan around as many of these difficulties as possible so that they do not threaten your business.

viii. Home based business ideas and low risk business ideas

Many people write to me and ask me for low risk business ideas. To me, most of the least risky businesses are on the web, which means that you can also work on them from home, and part-time if you have a full time job at the moment.

The reason these ideas are low-risk is that you don't need to pay for rent of physical space, you typically need fewer licenses and permits, and typically have to pay fewer employees. That takes quite a bit of financial risk out of the picture.

The simplest version of such a business is just a blog. A blog may seem like something that is too small and insignificant, but you can put up a blog in less than a day, and begin making money from it right away. And that is quite powerful. The blog can eventually outgrow itself and you can build a more interesting kind of a business around that website over time.

You Need A Website To Have A Web Based Business

Here is a tutorial for how to set up your blog in one day and get started. You can begin making money in less time than it would take you to finish the rest of this book!
http://www.problemio.com/website.html

If you are looking to have a web based business, you will certainly need a website. A website can be used to get people to discover your business, and then to sell to those people who are somewhere in the middle of the sales process. In the past, creating a website has been a challenge to many people, but it doesn't have to be difficult. You can set up a WordPress site in less than a day, and add an off the shelf theme to it to make it appear as a business site, and begin doing business that same day.

Choosing Your Business Niche

Before you rush to create a website, an arguably more difficult step in the process is to choose which business niche your website should focus on. Earlier in this book we discussed how to get business ideas. Try to follow some of those principles and choose a niche in which you are knowledgeable, experienced, and passionate, but also a niche that ultimately makes business sense.

How To Make Money From A Blog Or Website

The simplest way to make money from a blog or any other site is to put ads on that site. You can do that via Google's AdSense product. You can sign up for it here: http://www.google.com/adsense

Another way to make money on your site is to sell things from your site. You can sell things as an affiliate reseller which means that you will be selling products made by others. Or you can sell products that you create. Many people don't think of themselves as creators of products. But that is just a mental barrier. Everyone has some skills. The product doesn't have to be a physically tangible product. It can be a digital product like an e-book, or an educational product like this book, or a video-based online course that teaches something.

We'll get further into business models, revenue models and monetization strategies later in this book.

ix. Entrepreneur psychology: 7 important aspects

I want to share some observations about the common psychological issues related to starting and building a business.

People may wonder why this topic is present in this book, and the answer is that this is the most important topic in business that there can be. Why? Because your general psychology and the mindset with which you approach everything in your business is present 100% of the time. It affects every decision you make starting from your very first decision to even start your business. And that cannot be said about almost anything else. Maybe making money, doing marketing, or building a team may seem more important because they are more actionable and tangible. But your mental approach is equally important if not more so. Now let's get to some specific issues.

1) Positive Mental Approach vs. Finding Reasons You Can't Start

Before and after you start your business, you will face hundreds of difficulties, many of which may seem insurmountable. Some of the early difficulties may be things like having a lack of money, lack of experience, lack of time, lack of support, and possibly lack of general experience. These prevent many people from even starting their business.

Instead of focusing on reasons or excuses (no matter how legitimate they may seem) for why you are not able to get started, try to change how you think and talk about these things. For example, instead of starting a sentence with "I can't do thing xyz because…" try to think about how to get around that difficulty and form the sentence like "I am going to solve xyz by…" and the solution is up to you to figure out. Be creative and resourceful. The solution may not come to you right away, but keep hacking away at it. Believe in yourself and in the idea that you can solve that problem, and you will end up finding a way around that problem.

I will point out a great quote from Henry Ford:
"If you think you can do a thing, and you think you can't do a thing, you are right."

2) Keeping Your Ego In Check And Staying Humble

Building and growing a business can really boost a person's ego. After all, everyone tells you that you are great. You may have employees who have to agree with you because you are the boss. But you have to stay humble. Staying humble will keep you more likable and charismatic (which will make others more likely to naturally follow your lead) and will help you keep an open mind when hearing negative things about your business, or any of your decisions. That will help you absorb feedback faster which will in turn help you make changes within your business, and improve it more quickly.

Additionally, daydreaming about where your business will be in the future, getting press coverage, and constantly talking up your business can make you believe your own press and daydreams. Be careful of falling into that kind of a trap and don't begin believing your own press, daydreams of the future, or praise of friends. Most of us still have a lot to improve on, and to learn. We need to be humble and always look for ways to become better as people and business owners.

3) Dealing With Stress And Anxiety

Just about all entrepreneurs face stress and anxiety. The very nature of having a business almost facilitates the state of being under heavy stress. Every day, everything has to go right. Revenue must go up, the number of website visitors and customers must go up, the product has to improve, employees must be happy, customers must be happy, and much more. As the business owner, all of that rests on your shoulders. But there are almost no days where every aspect of your business is going to be perfect. Most days are closer to a two steps forward, one step back situation. There are even down periods which will feel like two steps back after only having taken one step forward. Some things go well and some things don't. And overall, things are probably moving more slowly than you would like. So you must prepare yourself for these days mentally, and not let the stress and anxiety build up if things don't go right. You must learn to be above the stress.

If you let those emotions get a hold of you, anxiety will affect your business decisions. And you do not want to have your business decisions influenced by stress and anxiety. Instead, you want to make well thought out decisions that are based on reason and discipline.

Sometimes what helps relieve stress and anxiety is the support of your family and friends. Regular exercise is also very good at helping you relieve stress and achieve mental health.

4) Dealing With Rejection And Failure

If you are growing your business and doing everything you can to make it a success, you will surely be dealing with frequent failure and rejection. It isn't because something is wrong, but because that is just the common occurrence for nearly every business. You will be pitching your business to potential investors, employees, customers, and others. Not everyone will like what you are doing. So get ready for some rejection.

The same is true about dealing with failure. If you are trying hard in marketing, building a quality product, growing revenue, and other things, some of your initiatives won't go exactly as you need them to go. That is OK. Things rarely work perfectly. In fact, the more common state of things is to encounter more failure than success. But as long as you are persistent, you will accumulate the successes, and build on them while learning from your failures.

Over time, rejection and failure hurts a bit more than the success you encounter. And these negative feelings can linger and build up. So just keep it in mind, and try to be in control of these emotions. Don't let them get to you as far as that is possible.

5) Be Prepared To Work Like You Have Never Worked Before

While it is fun to daydream about your business, once you begin working on it, the business will require incredible focus, long hours of hard work, discipline, and persistence. Keep that in mind. Those are not simple things which just happen as they need to happen. You are the one who will need to be doing much of the heavy lifting. As the business owner, most things will be on your shoulders. So just keep that in the back of your mind. Dreaming about a business and about one day being successful is fun. But actually creating this business is going to take amazingly hard work. So be ready to work harder than you've ever worked before.

6) Stay Motivated By Keeping A To-do List

Give yourself a list of daily tasks. The tasks should be somewhat simple so that you can keep crossing them off and adding new tasks. That will help you stay focused, organized, build momentum, and put you in a habit of moving the business forward every day.

7) Trust

When starting a business, many people become competitive to the point of losing all trust in people around them to the point of paranoia. This is observed most commonly when it comes to protecting business ideas. But it is important to be able to trust the people that we work with. You must make sure that you surround yourself with people whom you can trust so that you don' t close up mentally and emotionally, and can maintain a trusting and healthy business environment for you and your team.

x. Daydreaming about your business

Most entrepreneurs tend to dream and daydream about how great things will be after they make their business a success. Daydreaming about your success is a lot of fun. It is also tremendously inspiring and motivating. It often happens at random times and people find themselves happy and encouraged after waking up from a daydream where they imagine how great life will be after they build their business to be a great success.

But there is a trap here. In letting our imagination take over and tease us, that tease is so enticing that we can begin to believe parts of it while it is still quite early, and our business still quite young and new. And that can make us believe our wild imagination far before any of it is grounded in reality.

Once you begin to believe parts of the daydreams, it raises your ego and makes you feel like you are much closer to reaching your goals than you actually are. And that can cause you to develop an overconfidence, and make you relax a little bit because you are thinking that you are a big shot. But that is the exact wrong thing that you would want to happen because precisely at this time is when you need to be scrapping and working hard, not slowing down, but rather speeding up and adding intensity.

Daydreaming is fun, but don't allow it to convince you of success, or how great you are. Enjoy it when it happens because it really is fun and helps you stay motivated, but keep it in check and don't allow it to place false beliefs in your mind.

Daydreaming Distorts Reality Of How Hard You Will Need To Work

What I want to emphasize is that almost all entrepreneurs need to work extremely hard for a number of years before they find success. And what I often encounter is that people daydream and imagine how great things will be, and even build on top of those dreams in their imaginations. People often imagine how much money they will give to family and friends, what kind of car they will drive, how they will give back to charity and their community. But in none of these daydreams can be found anything about hard work and the daily grind that will be required to get to success.

Daydreaming Is Actually Important

Daydreaming is actually vital to healthy business psychology because it helps you envision yourself at a point where you reach success. A part of finding the confidence to succeed is to be able to see yourself being successful, and to believe that you can achieve success. If you can visualize it, it will be more concrete as a goal that you will be striving for. So daydreaming about your business is great. Just don't leave it at daydreaming, and don't get carried away with it. Make sure that you are actually taking real actionable steps to get to your eventual business success.

Don't Start A Business That Is Based On Dreams-Only

What I often encounter is that people try to start a business that is fully based on their dreams, but not much real-world research or experience. And that is dangerous. To start a business, you must be disciplined, know your market, and have experience in it. Your competitors will, and you have to as well.

xi. Negative attitudes that can destroy your business

Some of the common negative or bad attitudes that can hurt your business are having a high ego, convincing yourself of reasons not to start the business or being defeatist, and not being able to work well with people.

Having An Inflated Ego

As mentioned earlier, it is easy to fall into the trap of believing that you are so great. When we are daydreaming about business success, we are already on top of the world. In our daydreams, we made it! Even as you make progress with your business, every little success and step forward can be a great confidence and ego booster.

But it is important to realize that we are just at the beginning. Until we have made millions, or sold our companies, no matter how far along we think we are, the truth is that we are only at the beginning. We still have a lot to learn, and a lots of hard work ahead of us.

Having a big ego can make you seem like a know-it-all and make you stubborn. Neither of these is a sign of intelligence, and it will make you less likable. So be confident. Just don't get an inflated ego. Being humble also makes you more likable which is a great business advantage, especially for people in leadership roles.

Being Difficult To Work With

As a business founder, one of your most important skills is the ability to work well with people. Your investors, employees, advisers, and business partners should like and respect you, and enjoy working with you. If you can get them to like and respect you, it will be that much easier to get them all on-board with what you are doing.

You must lead by example without being stubborn or denigrating other people who work with you about not being as great as you are. You must listen to everyone, be strong in your opinion without being stubborn, and work to make everyone on your team better either by giving them projects in which they would excel, or by helping them.

It is really important to be a source of positivity on your team rather than a source of negativity. Negativity coming down from management tends to be very poisonous for the entire organization.

Having A Defeatist Attitude

When you are starting, or at any point of growing the business, make sure you have a can-do attitude. Try to catch your thoughts and see whether your mind pulls you in the direction of finding reasons why and how something can be made possible, or in the direction of finding reasons why that thing cannot be possible.

Very often, thoughts like having a lack of money, lack of experience, lack of support, or facing a number of other challenges can prevent and discourage you from starting the business. Don't let that kind of a mindset take over. It will stifle many of the initiatives which you want to undertake. Instead, try to be resourceful and creative about how to make things happen. Solutions for how to get around those difficulties won't necessarily come to you right away, or even that day. Some things may take weeks or months to figure out. But if you are persistent and are constantly working at finding a solution, you will be much more likely to find it.

xii. Checklist of items to determine whether your business idea is good

- Can you build this product or service?
- Do you have expertise in this business niche?
- Is the market too competitive for this business? And will you be able to compete?
- Is the market big enough for the business to achieve your financial goals for it?
- Does your target consumer have a good profile in terms of affluence and spending patterns?
- Are there natural channels through which to market this business?
- Do you have support of your family and those who are close to you with this business?
- Are you passionate about this idea?
- Would you want to do this business for many years?

xiii. How to think about building your product

Your product or service is arguably the most important aspect of your entire company. If you don't have a good product or service that your customers want, it will be extremely difficult to make sales. The product must accomplish two things:

1) It must be of some use (the more useful the better).
2) It must be of acceptable quality (the higher the quality, the better).

Sufficient Usefulness

There should be a good answer to the question of why this product or service should exist. The product or service should be of some benefit to someone or something. The product or service can solve a problem, entertain, educate, improve something, make some process easier or simpler, help save money or time, or anything else. For innovative new technology companies, this is sometimes not apparent. But for traditional services like lawn care or health services, the usefulness is very apparent.

Try to get a feel for exactly the thing that your company is going to make the world better with. If the company's product or service is unable pass this test, it probably should not exist, and you may need to change some part of your strategy.

Sufficient Quality

The product has to accomplish what it is meant to do with a sufficient degree of quality that is necessitated by the marketplace in which the company is meant to compete. The higher the quality of the product, the better it will fare in the marketplace, the more you can charge for it, and the happier your clients will be.

Additionally, it is important to note that quality is a relative term. You have to weigh the product quality of your company versus the quality of the products made by your competitors.

If, as a new company, if you find it difficult to be competitive in quality, try to find a part of the product which you can make better, or in a different enough way from your competitors to generate interest from consumers.

Part 3: PROTECTING YOUR INTELLECTUAL PROPERTY

i. 6 ways to protect intellectual property

Many people worry about having their business ideas stolen

or copied. In this chapter, we will go over some strategies to help protect your intellectual property. There are six different ways you can protect your intellectual property. They are patents, trademarks, copyrights, non disclosure agreements, non compete agreements, and very importantly, working with people whom you can trust.

It is important to make clear that I am not a lawyer and that in this chapter I only provide a practical high level overview of the relevant issues. In this book I do not give legal advice in any way, shape or form. If you need real legal help, please seek the advice of an attorney. Additionally, the legal concepts mentioned in this chapter apply to law in United States. If you are based in a different country, please research the business law that applies in the country in which you are based.

Patents

Patents are a legal tool designed to help protect your inventions. Inventions are new things that are already out there in the real world. That means you can't patent a business idea. Things you can patent are new designs, algorithms, gadgets, widgets, parts of or whole physical products, and even new kinds of food. But it must be a real and tangible thing. You can get a provisional patent in anticipation of something that you will invent, but for further details, please consult with an intellectual property lawyer.

Trademarks

Trademarks are intended to protect intellectual property such as logos, names, titles, or slogans. For example, the Nike "Just do it" slogan is something that is protected by a trademark. That means no other company can use that slogan. The Nike name is also protected by a trademark, and no other company can use that name either. The same goes for Nike's logo. Some trademarks apply only to particular industries and can be examined on a case by case basis. For further exploration of trademarks, please consult with an attorney.

Copyright

Copyright protects written works such as books, articles, blog posts, newspaper stories, and similar types of written works.

Non Disclosure Agreements (NDA)

The Non Disclosure Agreement is the most common legal tool to protect business ideas. The document can be either one-sided or two-sided. That means it can either protect the person who discloses the information (one-sided), or both parties (two-sided). The parties can be individuals, businesses, or nonprofits.

The problem with Non Disclosure Agreements is that in practice, they are less than ideal tools for protecting business ideas. To enforce the agreement, one must actually litigate. And to prove that an idea, or some information was stolen and used is not a simple thing to do.

Additionally, asking someone to sign an NDA is not always simple. Many people are averse to signing an NDA, and simply do not sign them. And when you ask someone to sign an NDA, it takes up their time, or the time the two of you have allocated for your meeting. That results in a part of the meeting being spent on the NDA rather than focusing on the actual business. Plus, discussing different philosophies and views about the NDA can sour the tone of the conversation. People tend to have strong views on this issue.

Non Compete Agreement

The Non Compete Agreement is typically used when hiring employees or adding someone to your team. It gives you protection in a few cases. It protects you from having your employees take your company secrets and going to work for your competitors. It also protects you from having your employees start their own businesses, and then stealing your clients or business secrets, and taking those clients or business secrets and using them to grow the businesses that they established.

Working With People You Can Trust

Keep in mind, to enforce any of the above legal tools, you actually have to litigate (go to court). That is time consuming, expensive, and not always fruitful or worthwhile. As you start and grow your business, always try to work with people you can trust, who have a reputation for being honest and honorable individuals and professionals.

Part 4: PLANNING YOUR BUSINESS IDEA

i. Do you need a business plan?

Many people write to me and ask whether they need a business plan. My answer is always simple. There are two instances when you should write a business plan. The first type of a situation in which you need a business plan is when some individual or organization that you want to work with, specifically asks for a business plan. The other type of a situation when you should write a business plan is for yourself to help you organize your ideas. Writing a business plan, even an informal one, can help you get your ideas organized, and your overall business model refined. The process of thinking about your business holistically, and considering every part of the business can help you catch and correct many mistakes before you start. It is much more expensive to realize that you are heading in a wrong direction after you have already started your business. So make sure you spend time planning your business and fixing potential problems in the overall business strategy as early as possible.

There are many benefits to writing the business plan just for yourself. First, you can have a single document where you and your business partners can agree on the structure, and execution of the details of the business. The other benefit is that it gives you something concrete where your ideas are laid out. You can use it to facilitate discussions within your team about each aspect of the business, and work to refine the various aspects of the business plan. This process will help you catch many potential pitfalls before you start your business.

Let's take a look at what exactly is a business plan.

What Is A Business Plan

I like to define the business plan as a document which expresses your business model and the execution of the business.

Did I just introduce another difficult term? Yes I did. Let's now take a look at what is a business model.

ii. What is a business model?

There are many different ways to look at what is a business model. Most of those are unnecessarily complex. So let me suggest a simple definition that we can use.

Business model definition - how every component of your business works on its own, and in relation to every other component of your business.

Let's unwrap that definition. The core point here is that when you look at a business, it is made up of many different parts. Some of the parts are marketing, creating and improving the actual product, the finances, the employees, the consumers that are targeted, and much more. And what is important in a business model is that all of these different aspects of a business are great individually while also working well with one another. This might sound simple in theory, but in practice, it is extremely difficult to come up with a great business model. As businesses are started and grown, the management team must constantly refine and improve every component of the business, and how those components work together.

The business model is not a static thing. It is something that evolves over time and gets better. And the better it can be during the planning phases of the business, the better off your business will be from the very beginning.

iii. How to write a business plan for your business idea

The sections below are the sections of a typical business plan. Each section has actionable tips for how to write and think about that particular section. Even if you are not writing a formal business plan, you must think deeply through each of the sections of a business plan before you start your business.

1) EXECUTIVE SUMMARY

This is a paragraph or two that acts as the introduction to your business plan. This is a general overview of the problem that your business is solving, the mission statement of the business. Prepare the reader for the issues you will cover in the rest of your business plan. You should briefly explain what your product is, but do not go into too much detail about the product. You will have a chance to get into details in subsequent sections.

2) YOUR PRODUCT OR SERVICE

This is the section where you should be more precise about your product. Explain your company's product or service. Is it a website? A physical store or service? A widget or a mobile app? What is special and unique about it?

Explain why this product or service should exist, and why it is needed. Does it entertain? Does it make someone feel better? Does it solve a problem for someone? Does it teach something? What is the benefit of this company? It may sound like a silly way to pose the question, but surprisingly many companies create a product or service that is not really needed, which causes difficulties when trying to sell it. Additionally, if your product or service is only needed a little bit, and doesn't solve a huge pain point or does not provide some great value, it may be difficult to get people to pay for it.

Lastly, but very importantly, explain how your product achieves what it promises to achieve. Don't leave that question unanswered.

3) WHAT STAGE OF THE BUSINESS ARE YOU IN?

Are you in the idea stage? Or have you started, and maybe you have a prototype? Or do you already have some revenue and a team?

Do not get into too many specifics here, but simply help the reader understand where you are in the process of building a company. It will help the reader have context within which to read the rest of the business plan.

It is OK to be at any stage, even the planning or the idea stage. Every large company has at some point been in planning stages.

4) WHO ARE YOUR TARGET USERS?

It is easy and tempting to think that everyone can use your product, but that would be a mistake. There are usually a few specific demographics for which your product will be a better fit. Having a focus on a particular consumer base will also help you better target your marketing and product usability efforts.

Especially in the beginning, try to understand who will be the best kind of a target users for your product. Usually there is a certain group, or a type of a customer that you have to win over to like your product. Once you identify your target consumer, effectively market to them, and get them to love your product, you can expand out to other demographics.

You have to define the demographics and psycho-graphics of this target consumer. Demographics are things like affluence level, education level, age, sex, geography of where they are located, and marital status. Psycho-graphics are things like needs, motivations, beliefs, hobbies, passions, etc.

WHAT NOT TO WRITE IN THIS SECTION: don't write something like everyone or all women or all men, or all people in some country or city. You have to show a much deeper understanding of your target consumer and their consumption behavior.

5) WHAT IS YOUR MARKET SIZE?

This is the total dollar amount of the industry in which your business is in. Some markets are multi-billion dollar markets, some markets total hundreds or tens of millions of dollars. You have to show that you understand what your market is, and its size.

If you are building a company that sells something very niche, your market size may be small, but if you are selling computers or cars, your market size is in the tens or hundreds of billions of dollars, and is obviously very large.

This section also shows the reader that you have done some due diligence and understand the business environment in which you are operating.

WHAT NOT TO WRITE IN THIS SECTION: don't simply write something like huge, very big, millions, or billions. You must research and know the statistics of your industry, and not just provide vague approximations.

You have to be as specific as possible with the dollar amount of your market size. The closer you can get to the actual dollar amount of the market size, the better.

6) MARKETING PLAN: HOW WILL YOU MARKET TO YOUR TARGET USERS?

There are many ways to market a product or service, but not all marketing techniques work for all companies, or to reach all kinds of people. Your marketing plan must outline how you will consistently reach your target market at scale, and convert them to clients.

For that reason, you have to craft your marketing plan very carefully. If your marketing plan is not a correct one, you may spend your time and money making misguided marketing efforts which would result on many months wasted without getting clients.

COMMON MISTAKE AND WHAT NOT TO SAY: If your marketing plan reads something like "I will market by posting on Facebook, Twitter, and handing out flyers and business cards" then you would be making a very common big mistake. If that sounds like your marketing strategy, that is not nearly enough. Your marketing plan must be much better.

I have created a number of resources to help you become better as a marketer. One of those resources is my marketing plan mobile apps on iOS and Android, and my second book which teaches you how to be a great marketer and reach 1,000,000 people. You can find all my marketing resources on Problemio.com if you feel that you may need marketing help. Additionally, my YouTube channel has over 10 hours of footage with different marketing tutorials.

7) REVENUE MODEL

In this section you must outline how, why and when there will be transactions which will bring you revenue. How many revenue streams will you have? What will be your single strongest revenue stream?

8) THE FINANCES

Before you start your business, and as you grow your business, you must have a clear view of the overall financial picture for your business. Maintaining a balance sheet or a cash flow statement can help you keep track of the overall financial picture of your business.

Large businesses typically have accountants who work on this section, but if your business is small, or you are just starting your business, you can create a basic cash flow statement, and that can be sufficient. We will cover cash flow statements later in this book.

9) UNIT ECONOMICS OVERVIEW

This is one of the most important sections of a business plan. This section outlines the details of each transaction. By focusing on the details of each transaction and looking at all possible transactions per day, month, or year, you can understand your entire financial model, and get a deep understand of the economics of your business. Understanding the anatomy of the finances of a single transaction can give you a great sense of what is working well, and what needs to be improved in the business.

This section tends to be one of the more intimidating sections of a business plan, so here is an example:

Imagine you are selling a widget. You sell the widget for a certain price, but it takes you some amount of time and money to produce, market, and sell the widget, while incurring costs like paying your employees, rent, and other bills. So there are revenue and expenses to consider. Expenses are easier to calculate because most of them are fixed. Some of them are employee salary, rent, and cost of the materials to produce the widgets.

You have to figure out what it costs you to put a widget into the customer's hands. And what you will charge for the widget? That is a single transaction. Once you dissect a single transaction this way, is it profitable? Or does it lose money? There is more to understanding unit economics, but for this introductory business plan tutorial, this is a good way to understand your unit economics.

Your job is to figure out the number of widgets you need to sell in order to 1) break even financially on a month to month basis, 2) turn a profit, 3) finance further business growth or your other goals.

You should also consider whether selling as many widgets as you need in order to meet your financial goals is viable through your available marketing channels and the size of your target market.

10) CURRENT TEAM

Provide brief professional backgrounds of each of the members of your executive team, and discuss the current size of the team. Explain why each team member's experience is the right fit for this business. Bonus points if the team has worked together before, and if members of the team have deep experience in the industry of the business. Additionally, if you have great mentors or advisers, you should add them to this section as well.

11) YOUR COMPETITION

It is important to understand and note who are the other players in your space. Your competitors are to be respected, understood, and learned from. You need to understand why they are successful as well as their shortcomings. Wherever they fail, may be an opportunity for your business to pick up and differentiate from them, and carve out a niche for your business. Wherever your competition is strong is an opportunity to learn from them. You do not need to be better than your competitors, but you do need to understand how your business will be different, and what section of the target market your approach may satisfy better. You also need to have strategies for competing with your competitors moving forward.

WHAT NOT TO DO: Don't over-focus or obsess about your competitors. There will always be someone competing with you. Understand and learn from your competitors, but focus on making your own business better. In the beginning, there are far more dangerous things than competition. New businesses are much more likely to die from basic implosion if they do not offer a great product or service, and sell it effectively.

12) PREVIOUS INVESTORS AND FUNDING

Give an overview of how your business has been funded so far. Depending on who will be reading your business plan, you can take out or add various sensitive information from this section.

Most entrepreneurs need and want to raise money. There are many potential ways to raise money. We will cover them in more detail later in this book.

13) WHAT ARE YOU LOOKING FOR?

If you are handing the business plan to someone, you may want to add a section explaining why you are writing the business plan. Are you raising money? Are you hiring employees? Or are you just gathering ideas on paper? If you are seeking something like funding or anything else, use this section as a good closing to your business plan. If the reader got this far, they are likely interested. So let them know how they can help.

iv. Different possible revenue models

There is a quite a bit of confusion about the terms revenue

model and revenue stream. They often get mixed with the term business model. As we covered earlier, a business model is something greater. A business model takes into account all your finances, how you get customers, the revenue streams that the business has, and much more. The revenue model is just a part of the business model. In this section, we will go over some of the most common revenue models and explain when and how they should be applied.

The Ad Revenue Model

The ad revenue model is the simplest revenue model. All you do is create an ad, place it on your website, billboard, or any other property, and you are set to go. But the truth is that your customers hate ads, and ignore them as much as possible. That makes ads so ineffective that they can only make a reasonable amount of money if the website, billboard, or whatever other media on which they are placed gets a very high volume of views. And the per view revenue is typically atrociously low.

On the web, the most common place to get ads which you can put on your website is Google's AdSense. For most sites, AdSense will earn somewhere from $5.00-$10.00 per 1,000 page views. A thousand page views is the common unit of measurement for ads. It is denoted by CPM.

If a typical CPM (cost per thousand views) is $5, then you need 10,000 views to make $50. And to make $500 you need 100,000 page views. And to make $5,000 which is getting close to the vicinity of a monthly salary for one person, you need to generate one million page views. All this means that your site needs to attract millions of people for you to be able to make any real money with ads. What you can do to increase your revenue potential is to think of another revenue stream that can work together with your ad revenue stream to improve results.

Affiliate Revenue Model

The affiliate revenue model is a very popular one, especially on the web. What it means is that you would be an affiliate reseller products or services provided by another company. This works on the web by having the affiliate reseller place links to relevant products on their website, and collecting commission on the generated sales.

This can work together in conjunction with ads, or separately. If you recall the section of this book about low-risk business ideas that you can do from home, becoming an affiliate reseller is perfect for that because all you need to get started with it is just a simple blog.

If you get it working well, selling affiliate products can sometimes make an order of magnitude more money than the ad-based revenue model. That isn't the case every time, and depends largely on your business niche, the kinds of products you are selling, and your audience. Pound for pound, the affiliate revenue model is a much stronger one than the ad-based revenue model.

Transactional Revenue Model

The transactional revenue model is the darling of all business owners because it is one of the most direct ways your business can get paid. You sell goods or provide a service, and people pay you for that. There is no need for ads, or referring people to some other affiliate websites, and waiting or hoping for sales to be made there. The challenge with this approach is that as soon as something can be sold for a profit, everyone jumps on the opportunity, and the business environment becomes crowded, making it difficult to market the business effectively, and bring in new customers at high volume.

Additionally, once there is competition, there begins to be price deterioration. And that causes everyone to make less money. The consumers love this because they get more options, and cheaper prices, but this is bad for your business because you ultimately make less money.

Nevertheless, if you can sell something, that is a great option to have. You just have to out-compete your competition. You can use the same blog on which you may be placing ads or reselling affiliate products, to sell whatever products of your own that you may be making.

Many people do not think of themselves as someone who can make a product, but I want to stop here for a second and make the argument that very likely, you *are* able to make a product that you can sell.

There are many different kinds of products. There are written works like this books or e-books that you can sell. There are arts and crafts that you can make at home and sell online. There are mobile apps or software products you can create. You can paint things, or make some kind of creative products. There are many different kinds of things you can make. Imagination is the limit. Just think of your talents. I am sure you will be able to come up with something great. An idea for a product may not come to you this very day, but if you think about it, a good idea for something you can create and sell will come to you sooner than you might think. Once you can create something, the great thing is that there is surely a way to sell it online.

Subscription Revenue Model

This is another darling of business owners. Not only does this mean recurring and somewhat predictable revenue, but it also means that revenue can accumulate every month as you grow your subscriber base.

If you can maintain a higher sign-up rate than your unsubscribe rate, you will have a beautiful revenue growth graph that is always up and to the right, with more subscribers and revenue each month.

Plus, the dirty little secret of subscription based revenue models is that many people simply don't unsubscribe because they are lazy or uncertain of whether they want to completely cut off the service. Think about how many people maintain their gym memberships, but have not been to the gym in months.

v. How to maximize your revenue streams

There are three common ways to maximize your revenue streams. You can maximize your revenue by charging more for your product, extending the duration of the relationship you have with each customer, and optimizing the rate at which new people are converted into paying customers. Let's explore each of these in more detail.

As a business owner, you always want to think about how to extend the lifetime relationship you have with your customers. Let's consider the example of buying a car. Does your relationship with that car dealer end there? It doesn't. The dealer lets you come in every 6 months for basic maintenance services and you get into a habit of going to that dealer. Then when it is time to buy your next car, you are likely going to consider buying from them again. If you look at almost any established business, you can notice a way in which that business tries to extend the lifetime of the relationships with its clients. Even my business does it. On my mobile apps there is an option to hire me as a business coach, and continue getting live mentoring from me as you grow your business.

Whether or not you are able to increase the duration of your relationship with your customers, you should also try to figure out how to charge more for your product or services. You can charge more by improving the quality of your offering, and by targeting a more affluent market in which people can afford to pay more for a higher level product or service. You can also add extra features to your product, which would enable you to raise the value of your product.

Lastly, what you should always be trying to do is to maximize the percentage of people who go from simply learning about your business to becoming paying clients of your business. To learn more about some strategies for how to do that, take a look at our next section about optimizing your sales funnel.

vi. How to optimize your sales funnel

Just about every business has a sales funnel. Improving the sales funnel improves the effectiveness of how your website or business converts people into paying clients. Optimizing your sales funnel can mean the difference between life and death for a business because the more effective your sales funnel is, the less money you have to spend on marketing your business in order to get the same amount of customers. That makes your average cost to acquire a customer lower, and your business more profitable overall.

Definition: What Is A Sales Funnel

A sales funnel is the series of steps that a person must take from when they first learn about your business to the point when they become a paying client.

When you are marketing your business and getting the word out about your business, you probably send people to your website or a physical location. That initial point where you tell people to go is the top of your sales funnel. And once people get to the top of your sales funnel, you need to have a very clear path for those people to progress through, in order to purchase something, or perform some action that you want them to do.

How To Improve The Sales Funnel: Measure Everything

If you drive people to your website, you must use web analytics software to measure and understand what those website visitors are doing on your website. The most common analytics software on the web is Google Analytics and it is free. Make sure that you use it to understand what your users are doing on your website if you are not already using it. If you are not familiar with web analytics, you definitely need to be. It will help your business quite a bit, and it is an industry standard.

Web analytics will help you understand what people are doing when they come to every page of your website. You need those website visitors to go to the next step of your sales funnel from whichever page they may be on. With analytics, you will be able to see whether people are making it to the next part of the sales funnel, and at what rate they are doing that. Knowing what your website visitors are already doing on your site will give you insight into how to adjust the site in order to get more of your website visitors to make the right steps to progress further in your sales funnel.

Test Everything To Optimize Your Sales Funnel

By now you may be asking how you can increase the rate at which people move forward through the sales funnel. What you have to do is define a clear call to action (usually a big button somewhere on the page) letting people know that this is where they need to go. Once you have added your call to action, try experimenting with where on that page the call to action should be, and what text should surround that call to action to make it more enticing for the website visitors to click it. You should also experiment with different layouts of the page to see what kind of a layout, color scheme, and usability might give you better results.

The best way to experiment is to use something called AB testing. AB testing is a testing technique in which you have two or more versions of a web page. You then drive people to both versions of that page, and test which of the web pages or designs generates a higher percentage of people performing that action that you want them to do.

The version of the page which works best to get users to do what you want them to do is the one you keep on your site.

Create Landing Pages

One way to improve your sales funnel is to shorten it. You can create a single page that is optimized for a single action that you want people to take. That kind of a page is called a landing page because once you create that page, you can drive people to land on it. It typically produces satisfactory results because prior to driving people to it, you are able to extensively test its effectiveness, and only drive people to it once you are satisfied with how effective it is.

Landing pages are a great tool to help you minimize the steps in your sales funnel, and therefore increase conversion of website visitors to buyers. Less steps means less people veering off the desired path in your sales funnel.

vii. Financials: the cash flow statement

The cash flow statement is a very important part of a business plan, and your business. For large companies, the cash flow statement tends to be very complex, and much of it is written by accountants. But if you are at the idea or planning stage of your business, it is simple and helpful to write your cash flow statement on your own. This section explains what is a cash flow statement, and how to write a basic cash flow statement for a new company.

Definition of Cash Flow Statement

A cash flow statement is a financial statement that shows how changes in balance sheet accounts and income affect cash (and cash equivalents), and breaks the analysis down to operating, investing, and financing activities. Essentially, the cash flow statement is concerned with the flow of cash in and out of the business. The statement captures both, the current operating results and the accompanying changes in the balance sheet.

That sounds complex, right? Let's simplify that definition. A cash flow statement for a new business is a glorified itemized list of ways cash is coming in and out of your business.

For new businesses, I recommend creating two such statements. The first cash flow statement will be for the time period before you open your business, and the second statement will have to do with cash flows after you open the business. Let's take a look at a small example.

Let's say that you are opening a restaurant in United States. First let's focus on the cash flow before the business is open.

Some (not all) of the cash flows *out* of the business are:

- Renting of the physical space
- Legal fees
- Salaries of some early employees
- Remodeling of the space

The cash flows *into* the business will be from funding sources like investments, loans, grants, donations etc.

Now let's focus on the cash flow statement after the business has started. Some (not all) of the cash flows out are:

- Monthly rent
- Employee salaries
- Utilities
- Liability insurance
- Ingredients for the food
- Marketing costs

And the cash flows *into* the business are the different revenue streams the business may have.

The reason that putting this document together is so important is that it gives you a clear sense of the financial picture for your business, and enable you to make financial projections. That enables you to understand how much money will be needed to start and run your business successfully.

When you pitch your business to investors, having created a cash flow statement, you will know exactly how much money to ask for. Depending on the type of business you have, you should give yourself 9-18 months of financial runway after the business has started.

viii. Freemium: Example of a popular business model and how to incorporate elements of it into your own business

Every business has to find, and over time refine, the kind of a business model that works best in their market and business environment. One of the common business model patterns is the Freemium business model. We can learn quite a bit from many of its elements.

Freemium Definition

Freemium - a business model that works by offering basic services, or a basic product for free, while charging a premium for advanced or special features. This particular business model has been used widely on the web, but it should not be limited to that. It is very common in the offline world as well.

How Freemium Works

Freemium has many variations, but the basic Freemium

pattern is to attract many people to something of value that is free, and charging for something at a certain point of the consumer's interaction with the free product. The reason this has been so successful on the web is that there is almost no cost for companies to give away digital goods since digital goods cost nothing to reproduce and give away.

Unlike physical goods which require physical materials, manufacturing, and need shipping, digital goods can be created over and over again by simply copying digital files. Compare that to a grocery store or a restaurant. These businesses cannot give away free goods because 1) their margins are too narrow and 2) there is a cost to getting each physical good into the store. Plus many people would rush to get the free food without paying, causing the stores or restaurants to quickly go out of business with this model.

Later in this section we will cover how even these types of businesses can and do use elements of the freemium business model to their advantage. But before we do that, let's expand the definition of freemium to include people who simply come to your site or into store or restaurant for free.

When you walk into a store, or sit down at a restaurant, you are a free user/customer. You may not buy anything in a store, and you may leave the restaurant without ordering (that is admittedly rare) or ordering menu items from which the restaurant owner makes no profit, but each business has some conversion rate of people who "convert" to customers from whom a profit can be made.

The more free visitors you have, the more paying customers you are likely to get because some of the non-paying people eventually convert to doing something profitable. Even if people never pay, they can bring their friends who pay, or they can leave nice online reviews (because they got everything for free or very cheap prices!) which will help you bring other people to your business. Even people who do not pay, or people who pay for something that is not profitable can be "re-purposed" to do something that will push your business forward.

Even on websites that make money with ads, all the visitors come to that website for free, and help the website indirectly make money by clicking on that site's ads. If you think about it, that is also a variation of the freemium model because the website attracts a mass of visitors by offering something of value for free, and then makes money when some of those people click on ads. The strict definition of freemium suggests that the free visitors are ultimately converted to paying customers. But as we see in this example, even if free visitors never pay a dime, elements of the freemium model are at play in many of these examples.

Do You Really Want Free Customers?

Free customers are actually not completely free. They often cost the business at least some money. Even if your business is a website, the business has to pay for servers to handle all the free traffic on the site. If it is a store, the non-paying visitors just make the store or restaurant more crowded for the paying customers and require some employee care. So why would a business want those non-paying people?

If you don't invite the free customers to your business, your competitors will. And some of those free customers will eventually convert to paying customers for your competitors. But that isn't even half of the problem. If your competitors get all the free customers, they will also get the word of mouth buzz and the social recommendations. Quickly, the consumer culture in your business space can shift to seeing your competitor as the best choice, and not you. Once that kind of a shift happens, it is difficult to reverse it. Plus, if you can attract everyone into your business whether they pay or not, that has the effect of suffocating your competitors because they do not get anyone visiting their stores or websites. And that is one of the best ways to kill off your competitors.

And don't forget, if your customers are not paying, that does not mean they are not beneficial to your business. Non-paying customers can help you spread the word about your business, and invite their friends. They can also possibly give your business good online reviews. There are many things they can do that can be helpful for your business. And non-paying customers do not have to remain that way. If you keep them engaged with your business, they may at some point warm up to the idea of spending money with your business, and become paying customers. Plus, as your product improves, something about your improved offering may also help them decide to begin spending money with your business.

Dealing With Low Conversion Rates And Mostly-Free Customers

Since most cases of the freemium model monetize rather poorly due to a high number of non-paying customers, what is a business owner to do in order to make reasonable revenue? The common answer is that the business owner has to attract a very high volume of non-paying customers in order to have a satisfactory number of people who eventually convert to paying clients. Reaching a very high volume of potential target customers is the goal with the freemium model. Additionally, you constantly have to work on improving and optimizing the conversion rate of people who convert from non paying visitors to paying customers.

ix. Identifying your target market

Understanding your target market and the behavior patterns of your potential consumers is one of the most important aspects of planning and running a business.

Understanding your consumer makes it easier and cheaper to reach them in large volume with targeted advertising. It also makes it easier to create a product that better satisfies their needs, and is used by them in a manner that is convenient to them (important for product adoption and customer retention). It also helps you better understand your market size which enables you to make more accurate financial estimates.

Targeting Is Not Limiting

A common misunderstanding is thinking that targeting a certain demographic limits the total opportunity of the business. There are two reasons why this is a misleading line of thought:

1) Choosing a target market helps you focus your advertising efforts and optimize your product to make that certain group very pleased with it. It still means that you will take anyone as a customer if they want to be your customer. You are not rejecting customers. But by targeting your target market, you are helping your business get the most out of a certain demographic of people who are best suited to be your customers.

2) If you start small with a sharper focus on a certain demographic, it does not mean you cannot grow bigger later. When your business is ready, you can target more

demographics as you expand.

Demographics And Psycho-graphics

When you identify your target market, you must identify it using demographics and psycho-graphics. Demographics are things like age, sex, affluence level, education level, where they live, etc. Psycho-graphics are things like interests, hobbies, motivations, moods, needs, etc. The more demographics and psycho-graphics you can pinpoint in your target consumers, the better.

Addressable Market vs. Overall Market

Within every market there is the total market, and then there is a subset of it that are more likely to become your customers.

The total available or addressable market is the entire market in which your business is in. The target market for your start-up is the part of that total market that your start-up can realistically target.

If, for example, you are opening a fine dining restaurant, the overall market for people who visit restaurants is probably everyone in your city. But your target market is much narrower. The actual market that you can realistically target is only those people who like to eat the certain kind of food found in your restaurant, who can afford to eat out instead of dining at home, and most likely who live within a 1-2 mile radius from your restaurant. Since in this example, we are discussing a fine dining restaurant, the target demographic may also be over 30 (or even 40) years old.

Here is another example. The total United States shoe market is in the billions of dollars per year. But if you made a shoe which is a slipper for men, you could only sell that to a portion of all men in United States.

It might be tempting to say that your target market is all men. But that is not true. Many men hate wearing slippers, and it is very difficult to force kids and teens to wear slippers. Men 25-45 years old largely do not like wearing slippers either, and many people prefer to walk around their homes barefoot. Older men tend to wear slippers at home, but as a demographic, they shop least often, and many elderly people live in poverty (or extreme saving mode), and can get items like slippers for free from various government help organizations. So it turns out that the people who would like your product the most, spend the least. And that is not a great situation.

The deeper you understand who behaves and spends in what particular ways, the better you will be able to estimate whom you can sell to, and identify a target market that can be lucrative and realistic to go after.

Additionally, if you had said that your target market for slippers was all men, and if you tried to market the slippers to all men, that would result in quite a bit of a wasted effort since reaching many of the men would do you no good since such a small subset of all men would buy the slippers.

Part 5: CREATING THE BUSINESS, AND BRINGING IT INTO REALITY

"Do what you can, with what you have, where you are."
- Theodore Roosevelt

i. Registering a new business

It is possible to simply wake up one day and start working on your business without registering it anywhere. That is not illegal, and no one is preventing anyone from doing that. But this approach has a few disadvantages. The main disadvantage is that you do not have liability protection of a business. That means that if someone sues you for something wrong you did while running your business, they will be suing you for your personal assets, and not the business. In order to get that liability protection in order not to be at risk of being sued for your personal possessions, you want to always do business as a legally registered business, and not as yourself.

Disclaimer: this book does not give legal advice. For legal advice, please contact an attorney.

In United States, the way to register your business is to go to the Secretary of State Office website for whatever state you are in, and go through the business registration process. Before you do that, you must decide on the type of business entity you want your business to be. I am not an attorney, and I don't give legal advice, and can't directly help you decide on the type of business entity you should choose.

Nevertheless, I conducted a series of video interviews with a professional in these issues. Here is the YouTube URL for a playlist of 9 videos where you can learn about how to properly register your business, and how to choose the right entity type for your business.

http://www.youtube.com/playlist?list=PLAgq5S6WQmzEK3W9nGc6z54Q5pHdKEg88

ii. Difference of a nonprofit and a for profit

There are many similarities between nonprofit organizations and for profit businesses. You register both with your state, and many laws apply to them in the same ways. Yet there are a few core fundamental differences between the two which we will outline in this section.

To become a nonprofit, the nonprofit has to prove that it is truly a nonprofit by satisfying a few criteria such as helping whatever cause they were established to help. After you register your nonprofit with the state, you still have to get a nonprofit status with the IRS because as a nonprofit, one of the biggest benefits you have is that you get some very big tax exemptions from the IRS.

Another difference between nonprofits and for profits is how they tend to raise money. Some nonprofits can be categorized as charitable trusts. And charitable trusts are much more likely to be donated to because to donate to a charity is a tax write-off. That is an important nuance because typically, wealthy individuals donate money in order to get tax write-offs. If a nonprofit is a charitable trust, one of the ways it is likely to raise money is from wealthy individuals who can make donations to them. Additionally, nonprofits are typically eligible for more types of grants and federal funding that for profit businesses can't get as readily.

The challenge with nonprofits is that they are limited in strategies they can take as a business because their focus needs to be on helping whatever cause they were established to help. It is often more difficult for nonprofits to generate revenue through their own means than it is for for-profit, simply because nonprofits have less strategy options at their disposal.

Another difference between nonprofits and for profit businesses is that for profit businesses are designed to distribute the profits to the company, or to its shareholders (the owners). In the case of non profits, while they are able to generate their own revenue, that revenue must go to supporting the longevity and sustainability of the nonprofit itself. And in case of nonprofits that are charities, all surplus revenue must be distributed by giving out that surplus revenue to the charities they are meant to support.

For nonprofits that are not charities, putting the surplus revenue into its own sustainability can mean paying extra to the founders or employees of the nonprofit. That becomes a very similar scenario as when a for profit business pays out extra revenue to its owners. So some of the differences between a nonprofit and for profit businesses can be a bit blurred at times.

iii. How to choose a business name

There are actually two business names that your business can have. The first name is the name you use when you register your business with the state. That is used for legal purposes. The second business name a business can have is used as its general brand. For example, my mobile apps and website are branded under the Problemio name. But that is not the name of the business which I registered with the state. You can change your company's brand name many times without having to change the name of the business that you registered with the state.

The business name that you must put thought into is your company's brand name that your customers will see. You must make sure that this name represents your business as you want your clients to perceive you. Many of the principles we will go over in this section also apply to how you should choose your website domain name, which is something we will focus on in the next section of this book.

First, make sure that your business name is not taken by another company, and is not trademarked. Before you decide on a particular name for your business, research the trademarks that are currently out there. Is the business name you want to choose already trademarked? If not, you may want to trademark your business name if you decide to use it. There are two benefits to trademarking your name. The first benefit is that you can prevent other companies from using your business name. The second benefit of trademarking your business name is that no new business can ever trademark that name and then be legally allowed to get you to stop using your name.

Here are some more quick tips to keep in mind as you

brainstorm potential brand names for your business.

- The business name must not be too long. One or two words is the max.
- The business name should be easy to remember.
- The business name should be easy to spell.
- The web address for the business name should not be taken.
- The business name should be easy to pronounce (you will be pronouncing it a lot! And you want others to easily pronounce it too) and should have a ring to it.
- The business name should not be too specific because your business strategy may change over time.
- The business name should give some hint of your overall brand without being too specific.

When you sit down to brainstorm your business name which will be your brand, try to do it with one or two other people so that you can bounce ideas off each other. Make a list of 50-100 potential names, and put them on a whiteboard so that all of them are visible. Try different variations and permutations of the different names together. As you brainstorm, consistently check whether the domain name for this brand name has been taken. It is very important to have your brand name and your website name be the same. Don't put pressure on yourself to come up with a business name on your first day of brainstorming. Give yourself time. This decision will have long-term consequences.

iv. How to choose a domain name for your website

Your website domain name is extremely important. It can help you with marketing, and it is a factor in how every visitor to your site perceives your brand. In fact, a domain name can play a very large role in whether or not people visit your site at all. Your domain name is often the first thing people learn about your site. You must make sure that your domain name makes a good first impression on them.

Checklist of Things To Do When Choosing Your Domain Name

- Create relatively short domain names.
- Preferably use a .com domain name.
- Use a domain name that is simple to spell.
- Use a domain name that is easy to also remember.
- The domain name should also be easy to pronounce.
- Use a domain name that gives some hint about what you are doing, but is not too specific. That will help you in case you have slight change in strategy in the future.

How To Tell Whether A Domain Name Is Available And How Much It Costs

Once you have an idea of what domain name you want, take a look at godaddy.com which offers a tool to check whether a domain name is taken, and how much it would cost to buy if it is available. Godaddy.com has a funny name, but it is one of the biggest and most reputable domain name registrars on the web.

What Not To Do When Choosing A Domain Name

- Make sure the domain name you choose does not come close to violating trademarks held by other companies. For example, do not get a domain name like facebooker.com because Facebook already owns the trademark on something very close, and can take legal action against your company.

- Do not make your domains too long to match an exact Google search phrase.
- Do not use hyphens in your name like this: boston-cleaners.com.
- Do not use numbers in your domain name (with rare exceptions).
- Avoid the .biz or .info domain names.

If you choose a domain name that ultimately isn't very good, that isn't the end of the world. If at some point in the future you will want to move to a different domain name, you can accomplish that with something called a 301 redirect. When you get a better domain name, redirect your existing site to render under the new domain name using a 301 redirect. There are challenges with this in that you will have to re-brand from scratch, and it will take a few days of work to move your site over to a new one. So only do this if you absolutely must. And don't do this many times. Try to come close to your optimal domain name from your first (or at worst a second) try.

v. What to look for in business partners, and where to find them

A good business partner can be an immense help when starting your business, but a bad business partner can damage your business quite a bit. In this section we will cover the traits to look for in a business partner, traits to avoid, and how to find good business partners.

What To Look For In Business Partners

There are a few professional and character traits that are an absolute must for good business partners. These are honesty, integrity, and being a pleasant person to work with. If the person you choose as your business person is not honest, that can cause severe problems down the road. Plus you will never be able to fully trust them. Remember, if the business succeeds, you will be partners for a very long time. So choose your business partners carefully.

The potential business partner must also be easy to get along with, and to work with. After all, you will be working together every day for a very long time. Together you need to form a strong team with good chemistry.

Additionally, it is extremely helpful if you and your business partner have worked together before. I realize that not everyone can get past co-workers to join them in their business venture, but if you have already worked together with your business partner in the past, statistically, the company has a greater chance of success.

Paul Graham of y-Combinator, which is the top start-up incubator in the world, always discusses how in his start-up incubator, teams that have worked together in the past tend to be more successful.

Another thing to look for in a business partner is that they have the same long-term and short-term goals as you do, and are equally passionate about the project.

And, of course, the business partner must bring something value to the business. Do they have many years of experience in the business niche in which the business idea is in? Do they possess a needed skill? What valuable assets does the business partner bring to the business? Additionally, look for them to have a proven track record of success.

What To Avoid In Business Partners

Some things to avoid in potential business partners are naturally some of the opposites of things you should look for. Avoid scheming and dishonest people. They will ruin your business like a cancer before the business even gets going. Always aim to do business with good, honest people who have integrity.

Additionally, and this is a debatable point, but I would suggest avoiding crazy people. Sometimes crazy can be brilliant, but you have to also consider what effect this person will have on the overall team. Make sure that your business partners can work well together with others.

Another thing to avoid when looking for potential business partners is hastily jumping into a partnership. As mentioned earlier, people who have worked together before have a greater chance to succeed. One thing you can do with a person with whom you have never worked with before is to set up a short trial period where you test out whether the two of you can make a good team and work well together.

Where And How To Find Business Partners

If you do not have a business partner, and need to find one who has some particular skills needed by your business, you can attend various industry events and network with people there. Once you start building business relationships, and expanding your business network, some potential business partners can come from the people you meet directly, or people to whom you may get introduced. Just remember, finding a great business partner is a long-term project. You will have to go to many networking events end explore many different options. You will have to truly focus on finding a business partner, and go through many people before finding the right one.

vi. Steve Blank's Customer Development Methodology & "Get out of the building"

Steve Blank is one of the most respected thinkers in the world of business today. Steve Blank is a Stanford business school professor, and an entrepreneur who has built multiple billion dollar companies earlier in his career. He is also an author of popular business books. Mr. Blank started in sales. He understood the power of talking to existing and potential customers about their current situation, their needs, and what would make their situations easier or simpler.

As Mr. Blank moved forward along his career path, his convictions about the benefits of talking to new and potential customers about their needs, were consistently supported by the results of his sales, and the sales departments of which he was in charge. He solidified and expressed his ideas in his Customer Development Methodology that is practiced by thousands of businesses today.

Let's explain that methodology. Imagine that you are starting a business to sell some service to some type of companies. During the planning phases of this business, you will surely be wondering whether this will be an easy service to sell, and how needed that service is to those kinds of companies. Certainly you hope that this will be an easy service to sell. But how do you really know? History shows that to act on your hope and assumptions is an incredibly faulty strategy which will increase the chances of your business not being successful. That is because as entrepreneurs, we are very hopeful and excited about our business. And that skews our perception of reality, and blinds us.

This is where the Customer Development Methodology kicks in and helps us. The Customer Development Methodology suggests that we should literally "get out of the building" and reach out to the people working at the companies to which we will be selling our products, and begin conversations with them about how painful the pain point we hope to solve really is. We should also discuss what their current solutions are to this pain point, and what they might look for in any other services that solve that pain point. You can also discuss how likely they will be to buy your product or services, and how much they would be able to pay.

Mind you, reaching out to the right people isn't easy or simple. Most of the people you reach out to will be busy and unwilling to help too much. It will also be a time consuming process filled with mediocre help, and rejection. But you must persevere and eventually find individuals who will be open to engage in dialog with you about the prospects of selling your products or services to their company.

You must talk to as many different such companies as you can. Plus, make sure that the individuals you talk to are not junior-level employees. Try to talk to people who can influence decisions, and who have a sufficient understanding of the needs of their business to give you reliable and insightful feedback. After you discuss the prospects of selling your product or service with many such companies, you will have done customer development, and your sense for your potential customer's needs will be keenly developed. You will also have a very clear view of whether your business idea is a viable one, and how easy or difficult it will be to sell the product or service that you are planning to provide.

vii. The Lean Start-up methodology by Eric Ries

Eric Ries is one of Steve Blank's most successful students, and was personally mentored by Steve Blank. Eric Ries is famous for his Lean Start-up methodology. It is easy to mistake the Lean Start-up for a basic suggestion to run your business in a lean way. But that isn't what this methodology is. The Lean Start-up methodology is a process that optimizes the rate at which you launch and improve your product. Let's dive into this a little deeper.

Let's use the example from the previous section of this book where we went through Steve Blank's Customer Development methodology. After doing customer development, a business can understand what kind of a product is needed by the businesses to which it will be trying to sell. That is great! Now you need to actually create this product. This is where the Lean Startup methodology largely takes over from the Customer Development methodology. I say largely because the truth is that throughout the lifetime of your business you should not stop practicing either of these methodologies because these are the best ways to maintain a deep understanding of your customers, and continue to evolve and improve your product.

The first part of the Lean Start-up methodology focuses on actually launching and releasing the first version of your product. A common mistake people make is to think up a very bulky product that is rich in features. But that adds product risk (remember product risk from an earlier chapter in this book?). The Lean Start-up dictates that you launch something called the Minimum Viable Product, also known as the MVP. Note that this is the minimal version of your product that is also viable. It is easy to just release something minimal. But don't forget the viable part of the equation. The product must work, and must be usable by your potential customers.

Once you release the Minimum Viable Product (MVP), you can quickly put that into the hands of your potential customers, and gather feedback about what they think about it, whether they would continue to use it, whether it is actually helpful to them, whether they would eventually pay money for something like this, and what may still be lacking in the product.

Keep in mind that almost no product was ever perfect in its first version. Don't expect your product to be perfect either. And don't be disappointed when people tell you what isn't very good about your product. If people tell you that the product is great, they are probably just not thinking about it hard enough. As you are gathering feedback about your MVP, try to understand where your product is lacking, and how you can improve it. Then quickly improve those parts of the product and release your updated product. Then get feedback all over again to understand new ways that your product is imperfect, and how to improve it. Throughout the lifetime of your business you will need to be constantly performing this cycle of feedback-gathering and product improvement. In the beginning stages of your business, the iterations may come in more rapid succession, and as your product and business mature, you may decrease the rate of iterations.

To give you a real world case study example, when I launched my first Problemio app on Android (where you are allowed to make as many app updates as you want and as quickly as you want), on some days I would release a new app update as often as 3 times per day because I was experimenting with which features the users of the app would like most. Over time the rate at which I updated that app slowed down to the current rate of about one every few weeks. To date, there have been nearly 200 big and small updates to my original app, and I never plan to completely stop updating the apps. There are always ways the apps can be improved. You will likely have a similar journey with your product, especially if it is a technology based product.

viii. How to pursue your idea if you have a full time job. Should you quit your job?

We all have to work to pay our rent. When people get struck with an interesting business idea, more likely than not, they are probably already working at a full time job or some job that helps them pay their rent. This puts them in a dilemma of whether they should pursue this fascinating idea, or spend most of their time at their job like they had been prior to getting this interesting idea. There is no simple solution. If they pursue the idea on their free time, which for most people is mornings, evenings, and weekends, their personal life suffers, and in any case, that time is really not enough to build a business. Plus, some of the most productive time of the week would be given to your job and not your business.

If people choose the other option, and quit their job, they take on a tremendous amount of financial risk, and add finance-related stress to their lives. Risk sounds fine as long as you imagine it, but you do not want to be on the bad outcome of a risky situation. It is not fun, and usually hits like a freight truck. So think long and carefully before you make such a decision.

Now let's talk about some possible solutions to this situation.

I'll start going over the solutions and possible options people have by noting a very common mistake I observe entrepreneurs making time and time again. In all their excitement, many hopeful entrepreneurs over-plan their business idea and pursue a complex business idea to which they can't devote much time or resources. If you have a job, and you are trying to pursue the business idea on your free time, try to simplify your business idea to make it simpler to bring to life. It doesn't have to remain simple forever. In fact, you should keep your big ambitions, and not lose sight of them. Keeping your big plans in mind will be one of the keys to help you stay motivated. But figure out a way to start small so that you can actually get started.

Additionally, if you have a full-time job, you can put some of the money you earn at your job to pay freelance workers who can help you accomplish tasks needed by your business. That way you can hire reasonably priced help without having to risk your job.

Lastly, all entrepreneurs have limited resources (time, money, skilled labor), but if you have a full-time job, you have even less time. Try to prioritize the tasks that you need to get done. Staying very focused on growing that simple business and improving its product, will go a long way in helping you maximize the time you have available to devote to your business.

A great option is to get experienced mentors who can help you understand which tasks should be prioritized, and what strategies your business should pursue. A poorly chosen strategy can cost you months of effort. If you can get the help and support to help you stay on the right track, that will also go a long way in helping you grow your business.

Before I end this section, I want to make an important note

about handling your full-time job and your business. Do not use your work time, or work equipment to work on your business without the permission of your boss at work. You don't have to tell your employer that you are pursuing a business on the side, but if you plan to use the employer's facilities or equipment, get their permission. Additionally, if you ever signed a non compete agreement with your employer, make sure you honor that.

ix. Starting a business with no experience. Should you? How to pull it off?

In this section we will go over the pros and cons of starting a business with no experience, and cover some things you can do to increase your chance of success even if you have limited experience as an entrepreneur or in a certain business niche.

It Is Better To Have Experience

It is certainly better to have experience than not having it. Experience can help you choose a stronger overall business strategy, and give you a stronger sense for what business direction may be more fruitful. Experience can also help you avoid some of the common mistakes which have the potential to derail your business, or waste resources. If you do not have a great amount of experience in business, or within your business idea niche, it is not an optimal situation, but it is also not the end of the world. What you will need to do to compensate for your lack of experience by building a team around you which does have the necessary experience. The team can be your business partners, mentors, investors, or advisers.

Get Mentors And Advisers

Having great mentors and advisers is a crucial component to building a successful business. Entrepreneurs (especially first-time entrepreneurs or young entrepreneurs) should seek out mentors or advisers. But don't just seek out any mentor who tells you that they understand business. A quality mentor must satisfy a few criteria.

The first criteria is that this potential mentor must have started and built a successful business before. It is even better if the business that they previously built is in the same business niche as your current business. The next criteria is that this mentor must have an incentive for you to succeed. People approach things much differently when their own money or future is on the line. If you find a great potential mentor or an advisor, you can offer them equity in your business to get them motivated. Another criteria for a potential mentor is that they do not look down on you as too inexperienced, and that they do not have an ego. They must respect your ideas even though their ideas are probably better. Lastly, a potential mentor must also be a good teacher because they will need to have the patience to explain many things to you along the way.

Someone On Your Team Needs Experience

Even if you do find great mentors, when you build your team, you should make sure that the team members you bring on, have complimenting skill sets to each other. Of course, if you have a tech start-up, most people should have a technology background. But you should also have at least one person who understands business, branding, and marketing to help guide the work of the developers.

Extremely Hard Work Can Compensate For Lack Of Experience

With hard work, you can move mountains and achieve the impossible. Hard work and hunger can compensate for what you might lack in experience. But there is no reason to approach your business solely with hard work. Hard work is an absolute must in any business, and is the base minimum. Try to also supplement it with savvy and experience by building an experienced team around you. Hard work together with experience is optimal.

Do You Need A Degree To Start A Business?

Many people also ask whether a business degree is necessary to start a business. While a degree is not a legal requirement to start a business, getting a degree is one way to gain experience in a number of different fields. The degree does not have to be in business. A Computer Science degree can help you become a software developer and empower you to build products. A writing degree can help you build written products (books, eBooks, blogs, etc). There are many different skills that a degree can give you. That makes the question of whether someone should get a degree before they start a business somewhat incorrect. A degree can help quite a bit. But it isn't a hard requirement to start a business.

x. Importance of getting a business mentor, and how to get a mentor

In proper business theory, every CEO should have a CEO coach, advisor, or mentor. They should meet either once a week, twice a week, or once a month. The coach can help brainstorm strategy, give feedback on various upcoming business decisions, and simply listen if the entrepreneur needs to vent some frustrations.

Experienced entrepreneurs understand the importance of having a mentor or a coach because when they look back at their own experience of growing their companies, they see many instances when they made mistakes that could have been prevented by some very simple advice. Experienced entrepreneurs also understand that business mistakes can be extremely costly. If you choose an incorrect strategy, it can take months of wasted time to execute that strategy, measure the results, realize that this strategy was faulty, brainstorm a new strategy, and start executing that new strategy.

We all hope that this wouldn't happen to us. But this happens to almost everyone. And it tends to happen multiple times throughout people's careers as entrepreneurs. Experienced entrepreneurs think back to those mistakes and understand that if only they had a mentor who could have advised them, and steered them clear of that mistake, they would have been far better off. First-time entrepreneurs don't have the benefit of that experience, and most first-time entrepreneurs don't ever get a mentor, naively hoping that they won't make those types of costly and preventable mistakes.

How To Get A Business Mentor

The best mentors are ones who have successfully built a business in your business niche, who want you to succeed, with whom you can develop a good working relationship and a working chemistry, and who have time to devote to meeting with you on a regular basis.

A person who fits all these criteria is extremely difficult to find. Most entrepreneurs never find such a great mentor or coach. If they do find such a person, their services are usually not free, and are quite expensive because many people want the help of that person. If you can get someone who has at least some of those qualities to mentor you for free, that person can still help you tremendously.

To find such a mentor, research some of the successful (or at least operational) companies in your business niche. Then reach out to the CEOs or senior employees in those companies. Don't ask to get mentored right away. That will just result in quickly getting rejected. First, just begin business relationships with those people. Try to show humility, and an interest in learning. Additionally, as simple as it may sound, everyone likes it when you compliment something about them and their business. If you find that some of the people to whom you have reached out are responsive, and you have positive interactions with them, ask them to meet over coffee, or in their office. Remember, when you ask them to meet, offer to meet whenever it is convenient for them, for a short time, and at a location that is convenient for them. That is generally the right practice of asking people to meet from whom you are seeking advice or business help.

There is a small trick here. If you ask for a five minute meeting, most people can pencil you into their schedules almost no matter how busy their schedule may be. But if the two of you hit it off, and have an engaging conversation, that five minutes can naturally grow to ten, twenty, or thirty minutes. And if it turns out that there is really not much to discuss, then five minutes is just right because you can get in and get out without taking up much of that person's time.

Most people will be simply too busy to help. I can share a personal case study. After having gotten hundreds of thousands of downloads to my Problemio mobile apps which help entrepreneurs start their businesses, and over a hundred thousand views on my business YouTube channel, you can imagine how many people email me asking me to become their mentor. I get up to 50 such emails per week. While I would love to help everyone, I can't possibly help everyone who asks me for help as a mentor. I am always happy to answer quick questions because that only takes me about a minute or two, but when someone asks to mentor them, which is something that would require hours, I am forced to charge them a consulting fee to determine how committed and serious they are. But there are some people whom I do help. Those people tend to be ones who ask something insightful, or compliment some of my products, or offer to help me in some capacity. And that is an important point. Don't be a taker. Offer to help with something first.

The same situation that I just described may be the case with the people whom you will ask to be your mentors. They might want to help, but simply not have the time to devote to you in order to truly be of help. In fact, most experienced entrepreneurs love to help new entrepreneurs because they realize how difficult it is to be a new entrepreneur since at one point they themselves were new entrepreneurs. Most experienced entrepreneurs do try to help new entrepreneurs when they can. But they just don't have the time to help everyone who needs help. They need a filter to figure out whom to help, and whom to turn away.

So you must contact many people, and very importantly, don't ask for favors right away. Forge business relationships first. Otherwise, you will be one of many people who ask something without first offering to help in any way, and they will send you to the back of that long line of people who ask them for things, but themselves bring no value to them.

If You Can't Get A Mentor, Build A Network Of Peers

Whether you are able to get a mentor, or not, you should always be looking to build a strong network of your peers who are other entrepreneurs, or professionals within your business niche. The relationship you want to forge and maintain with them should be one of mutual help. If you need advice or a bit of help, you should be able to reach out to your network of peers, and get the help you need. But the only way you can consistently rely on people's help is if you consistently help them when they need the help.

xi. When to hire a lawyer, accountant, and get business liability insurance

Many people wonder when they should seek the help of a lawyer, an accountant, and get liability insurance for their business. Let's examine when you should begin exploring your options with each of these.

It is best if you consult with a lawyer before you start your business. Lawyers tend to give free initial consultations, and they understand that in the beginning, you simply need advice. In your initial conversations, you can talk to an intellectual property lawyer to help you understand whether patents, trademarks, or any other legal options may be right for you. You can also talk to a general business lawyer to help you understand what kind of a business entity (LLC, S corp, C corp, or any other type of business entity) may be right for you.

You should also consult with an accountant who specializes in working with businesses. The accountant can also advise you on the type of business entity you should choose. Additionally, the accountant can help you understand the tax implications of your decisions.

When it comes to getting business insurance, things vary depending on the industry in which you are in. If you are in construction, trucking industries, or any industry where the rate of accidents is high, you should definitely look to get liability insurance for your business. And if you are in industries where there is less of a chance of you getting sued, your insurance costs may be lower. If you can afford it, it may be a good idea to buy insurance for your business. You never know what can happen, and it is a good idea to protect the business which you worked so hard to build. Ultimately, whether you do or do not get business insurance, it is a business decision that is up to you depending on how much risk and expenses you are willing to take on.

Keep in mind that you have options for getting legal and accounting help. If you can afford it, you can simply pay the lawyer and the accountant to help you with your legal and tax issues. Those are relatively expensive options for someone who is just starting their business. But it is also the option with which you are most likely to get the highest quality service. If you don't have the money to pay for everything, there are DIY (Do It Yourself) options through things like legalzoom.com and various tax software. There will be a learning curve for learning to use those DIY tools, and chances are that what you will be able to accomplish will not be equally as good as a lawyer and an accountant would accomplish, but the costs will be orders of magnitude lower than hiring a lawyer and an accountant. The option you choose depends largely on the financial resources you have available to you. When your business grows, and you can afford to pay the lawyer and the accountant, you can reach out to those professionals who originally helped you, and finally hire them to help your business.

xii. The fail fast to succeed faster methodology

We have already explored the Customer Development methodology from Steve Blank, and the Lean Start-up methodology from Eric Ries. Now let's explore a third type of methodology (last one, I promise!) which is the Fail Fast, Succeed Faster methodology.

This methodology is especially useful for innovative business ideas. Here is the logic behind the catchy name. When you are an innovative business or a start-up, you operate on many premises which have not yet been proven. Your premises are essentially educated guesses. When you start, you really don't know whether your business idea will work the way you hope. That is why it is innovative. It is up to you to forge your way, and make this new kind of a business idea work out. The innovative process is a series of attempts on your part to see whether your initial estimates and assumptions for how things would work out, would be confirmed by real-world tests.

As you innovate, most of your efforts will be trial and error attempts. Most of these will not work out. These will be small failures. That is OK, and completely expected. In fact, if you said that you started an innovative business, and had no failures along the way, I would question either how truly innovative that business is, or whether you are understating the failures you encountered along the way. Most people have far more failures than successes.

The trick is to experiment rapidly to learn from the failures (fail fast), and accumulate the small successes along the way (to succeed faster). Whenever you see that some small experiment didn't fail, and had positive results, you can build on top of that. And that is why this methodology is called fail fast, and succeed faster. The more rapidly you innovate and try different things, the faster you will learn what is working and what is not working.

xiii. Skills you will need to make your business a success

There are some skills which will help you build your company. You may be thinking about particular day to day skills needed by the business to accomplish various tasks. Sometimes those skills are referred to as hard skills. But this section covers some soft skills like personality traits and aptitudes. Let's go over a few examples.

Persistence

Persistence is probably the single most important skill that you will need to make your business a success. Almost nothing you will try will work on the very first attempt. As I mentioned earlier in, my original mobile app has gone through approximately 200 iterations. Many of those iterations were aimed at achieving a particular result. And many of those iterations failed. You can imagine that it was often a very frustrating and disappointing experience. But only because I stuck with it, and kept trying different things, I eventually achieved what I wanted to achieve with the app.

Hard Work

Hard work is another skill that you will need to bring to your business. In fact, hard work and persistence go hand in hand, and I was torn which of these should be first on this list.

Hard work is probably an understatement. Incredibly hard work is more like it. Most small business owners work six to seven days a week, and on most days the work day is longer than ten hours. My personal work days are even longer than that. There is a lot to do, and as the business owner, it is your responsibility to get it all done. You can relax your work schedule a little bit once your business matures because that work schedule is not sustainable over a long time, but in the beginning, as you are making the business happen by literally willing it into existence with all your efforts, the business will require you to work incredibly hard.

Resourcefulness And Creativity

When you start your business, in most cases you will have a very limited amount of money with which to accomplish the many things that the business will need to accomplish. Even if you had unlimited amounts of money to throw at problems, it often wouldn't actually solve that problem. And it is important not to waste money because even if you raise it once, it is difficult to raise money again without having made great progress with your business.

You will need to be creative and resourceful in how you get mentors, build your product, do your marketing and advertising, get great people to work with you, and get many costly things accomplished cheaply or for free.

Charisma

You will need to be a great leader because you will need your employees to follow your lead, your business partners to want to partner with you, and your mentors and investors to see you as a person who can build a great team, and a great business. You will also need to be charismatic when doing sales and marketing, and interacting with everyone. Very often, the personal brand of the CEO or founder of a business becomes closely associated to the overall brand of the business. For example, even if my own business is just mobile apps, and I do not need to be the face of the business, to promote the apps, I created a YouTube channel where I appear in hundreds of videos, and a podcast where my listeners get to know me. I also speak at events, and am pushing the business wherever I can. If, as the founder, you become the face of the company. That can help your marketing efforts quite a bit. That means you must learn to be (or already be) charismatic.

xiv. More tips for early-stage businesses

It can take a number of years to grow from the idea stage to whatever the eventual end point may be. The stages of a company can be broken down into many parts. The first stage is the planning stage.

The Planning Stage

This is when you are thinking about the product, the company, and overall strategy. Here are some important questions to consider when evaluating a concept company or a company idea:

1) What is the product? Is it needed in the world?
2) Who is the target customer? What are the behavior patterns of the target consumers, and will they like to use the

product in the way that you are thinking about making the product?

3) Can the target customer be easily reached in large numbers, and marketed to?

4) How can money be made from this product or service? Is the business model viable?

5) Do you, as the founder of this business, add any competitive advantage? Do you have expertise or connections that might help this business?

6) Are you able to build the product that is necessary? Or will the product require investment funds? If the company requires outside money to reach success, will you be able to raise that money?

7) Is this something you really want to do for the next few years?

8) How big of a pain point is the business solving? Is the pain point a very painful one? The bigger the point point you are solving the better because that means your consumers will make more of an effort to have that need met.

There are many more such considerations. It is important that every part of the strategy takes other parts of the strategy into consideration, and they all work well together to form a very strong business model. Sometimes one part of the strategy needs to be changed, and that causes many of the other parts of the strategy to no longer work. So be careful of that.

During the planning stage, the goal is to think through, and gain a deep understanding of every facet of your company, and overall strategy. You must evaluate whether the plan as a whole is viable, or whether there are big difficulties ahead that need to be accounted for. Foresight is the key during the planning phase.

Cheaply Validating The Business Idea

Once you have thought through the idea, and still like the idea, it might seem that the next step is to go ahead and create that product, or start providing that service. But that often requires substantial capital. If you want to minimize your risk, some practical things to do are:

1) Talk to as many people about your idea as possible and get their opinions.

2) Reach out to people who work in the industry, and try to get their opinions or knowledge about the industry. If you can, get them to become mentors. Mentors have a way of sometimes becoming investors or partners as the business picks up momentum.

3) Do market research, industry projections research, and competitor research.

4) Try your business idea on a small scale. For example, if you have a food product, try to sell it from a cart or at fairs to get a sense for the demand. If you have a physical product, try to sell it at small stores before you have tens of thousands units manufactured. This will give you real world sales metrics on which you can base future decisions. That is significantly better than basing big financial decisions on unproven theory.

Validating The Idea In The Market

The next stage after you have a solid plan is to turn that plan from theory to reality. The question now becomes one of how to put the first version of the product out in front of real users to see how they respond to the product or service.

First, you must build a founding team that can create the first version of your product or enable whatever service you are planning to provide. Here, Eric Ries is the thought leader on how to bring the minimum viable product (MVP) to market.

The great thing about the minimum viable product is that it focuses on bringing the product to market sooner rather than later. Once you have your minimum viable product (MVP) in front of users or customers, you can see how it performs in the real world. If users love it, that is great. If they do not, you can learn why not, and make consistent improvements to your product until they like it better. The beauty of the MVP model is that it enables you to iterate quickly while learning the most about how your users react to your product or service.

Once you have your product in the market and in front of customers, continue improving it until it becomes great, and begins to get market adoption, or the opposite happens and you realize that the market has rejected your approach. Either way, following the MVP approach, you will get there faster and cheaper.

Just make sure that when you let people try your product that those people are actually in your target market, and not some random friends who have little use for this product.

Additionally, friends and family tend to say that they like your product just to make you feel better. Even though it is tempting to listen to praise, don't listen to them too much. What you need is constructive and objective feedback.
The goal is to have the market tell you whether your idea is good or not.

xv. Timeline with steps for how to

start your business

While there is no single possible timeline that fits all businesses, the timeline suggested here is composed of fundamentally good-practice techniques. It is up to you to decide the exact order of the steps outlined below.

Step One: Get A Business Idea

First, you need some idea of what your business should be. Presumably, since you have made it this far in the book, you already have a business idea. So we won't spend much time here. Plus, there are other sections of this book devoted to getting business ideas.

Step Two: Learn To Pitch And Explain Your Business

Just as there are other sections in this book devoted to getting business ideas, there is a section of this book devoted to pitching your business. I'll only mention that the reason it is important to learn to pitch your idea so early is that you will need to be able to explain it to others in a way that is clear, to make sure they understand what you are trying to explain.

Step Three: Get Feedback About Your Idea From Others

Once you can communicate your business idea in a clear and effective way, you can begin to ask others for feedback. In the early stage of a business, as a rule of thumb, you want to get as much feedback and opinions from people as possible. You do not have to act on all the suggestions and opinions, but it is good to listen to many different types of feedback and perspectives to help solidify your own vision of your project, and get signals for where you may be on the wrong track so that you can fix whatever you are doing wrong early.

NOTE: You should also research the history of this idea. Has it been tried before? To what degree of success, and how many times? What difficulties did the past attempts encounter? And can you overcome or sidestep those difficulties with your approach? Try to learn from the mistakes of others. It is the cheapest way to learn, and it can give you many good ideas for your venture. Plus it will make you more aware of the issues associated with your business.

Step Four: What To Do If Not All Market Research Is Positive

It is perfectly normal to get some negative feedback and market test results. In fact, this should happen if you are doing a good job of gathering feedback. No idea is perfect from the start. There are many details about your initial business idea and product that will need to be refined throughout the lifetime of the company. Here is how to go about refining your idea while making sure you keep yourself and the company focused. You can create a company mission statement. Your company can have a stable overall mission that it strives for, while how you go about accomplishing it can change according to whatever strategy makes the most sense.

Here is an example of a possible company mission statement: we will improve history education for kids k-12. Here are possible plans for how that goal can be achieved: 1) Write better books and sell them to schools 2) Create iPad apps and provide schools with iPads 3) Work to have higher salaries for teachers, which would improve education quality. Notice that the goal of the business remains the same while the strategy for how that goal can be accomplished can change completely in order to find a strategy that is actually viable when it comes to executing it, and making it work.

Step Five: What To Do If All Market Tests Are Positive

If all signs point in the right direction, and you are still enthusiastic about the project, then it is time to begin thinking about turning this idea into a real company.

One of the first things you will need to consider is the type of company formation you need to have (Sole Proprietor, LLC, C, S, etc), and other legal issues. It is a good idea to consult an attorney who is qualified to help you understand the basic company legal needs such as an NDA agreement, trademarks, employee and contractor agreements, and agreements between you and your partners if you have any.

Once you have registered your business, you are ready to grow it. That means focusing on constantly improving your product quality, and marketing to get clients. Check the last chapter of this book for further resources on marketing, and growing your business. Your humble author has created hundreds of YouTube video tutorials for just about every part of growing your business.

Step By Step: A Comprehensive Guide

Part 6: RAISING MONEY FOR YOUR BUSINESS

"We raise money every day, from our customers."
— Sahil Lavingia

i. How much money you should raise to start your business

On my apps, many people ask me how they can determine how much money they need to raise to start their business. Of course, the answer is that it depends. Don't you just love those types of answers? In this case, it is true because businesses can be so different from one another. The answer depends on many factors, so instead of providing some high-level answer that would not be too helpful, I'll explain the steps you can take to calculate the cost of starting your particular business. That will allow you to determine how much money you will need to raise in order to start your unique business.

Cash Flow Analysis To Help Understand How Much Money Is Needed

We covered how to create a cash flow statement for a new business in an earlier chapter. When you raise money, you must know how much money you will need to raise in order to get to some goal for the business. The goal can be a certain level of profits, certain number of users or any other milestone that will be crucial to get to. You should estimate how long it will take you in order to get to that goal. Doing cash flow analysis can be used to project how much money will be needed to get to that goal, and will give you an idea of how much money you will need to raise.

If you are just starting your business, you usually want to give yourself about 6-18 months of runway before you run out of money. And just because entrepreneurs tend to be overly optimistic about the prospects of their business, they can often underestimate how difficult things might be. So adding 15-30% on top of your estimated financial needs can often be a reasonable thing to do, and can give you an extra financial cushion.

Raising The Money You Need

Once you know how much money you need to raise, you can begin looking into ways to raise that money.

The 8 sources of raising money we discuss in this chapter are loans, grants, investments, donations, revenue of your actual business, creative fundraising techniques, getting the money upfront from potential customers, and working a side job to fund the business.

Additionally, if you are based in United States, you can take a look at government sites like grants.gov or sba.gov to see whether they can be of help to you. If you are not based in United States, there are probably equivalent sites for your country, so just look up what those are for the country where you live.

What If You Can't Raise The Money You Need To Start Your Business

Unfortunately, most people never end up getting the money they need to start their small business. Raising money is a very difficult process. This causes many people to abandon their dreams. But it doesn't have to be that way. I want to introduce the concept of bootstrapping which is a way to create and grow your business without needing much money. Bootstrapping is as much a methodology (this one is truly the last one, I promise) as much as it is a mindset, coupled with a number of tactics you can use to build your business despite not having the financial resources.

ii. Bootstrapping: how to start your business without much money

An overwhelming number of people who write to me asking about how they can start a business, ask specifically about how they can start a business if they have no money to put into it, and no real ways to raise that money.

Of course, it is much simpler to start a business if you do have money, but many people start successful businesses without any money all the time. In most cases, a lack of money shouldn't stop you. In this section I will explain how you can start a business with no money, and no funding by successfully bootstrapping your business.

Definition Of Bootstrapping

Bootstrapping usually refers to the starting of a self-sustaining business that is supposed to proceed without external financial input. This term does not have to apply to business situations only. But when this term is used in business, it refers to the process of starting and growing a business without an outside cash injection. Such business are typically funded by the founder, or are able to quickly generate revenue by getting paying customers. That can sustain the operations of the business long-term because it promotes solid business fundamentals.

Most Entrepreneurs Do Not Have Money

Almost every entrepreneur has to face the problem of not having enough money (in many cases no money at all) to help them accomplish the things they need to accomplish in order to grow their business. If you find yourself feeling like you don't have the money to start your business, don't worry, you are not alone. In fact, you are a part of an overwhelming majority of entrepreneurs. There are many lessons we can learn from entrepreneurs who have started and built their businesses with little or no money. The single most important lesson is that it is possible. Entrepreneurs who succeed are usually ones who are persistent and resourceful. So don't lose confidence. Just be resourceful and figure out how to get around your money issues. History shows that it is completely possible to overcome the problem of not having much money to start your business. In fact, going through that experience will make you much stronger as an entrepreneur.

Start A Business By Bootstrapping

Most entrepreneurs start a business by simply bootstrapping it. Bootstrapping almost forces the entrepreneur to be resourceful and to take on a can-do mindset which helps them find ways for doing everything cheaply or for free by using their resourcefulness and creativity. Knowing that they can't afford to pay for most things puts the entrepreneur with their back against the wall, and forces them to find ways to "wiggle out" of whatever challenges they are facing.

Let me share a case study example from my own experience as an entrepreneur. When I started my mobile app business problemio.com, I started it with no money. That meant I could not hire employees, could not pay for a nice design for my business, had to build the product, do the marketing and sales, and everything else that the business required. Since I didn't have a co-founder or a business partner who could help me with some of those tasks, it meant that I had to learn many of the skill sets that were needed by the business.

Of course, I could not do many of the tasks that I needed to a very high degree of quality. For example, design was a very difficult thing for me to learn. But I was able to learn most of the other skills needed by the business to be able to perform them at approximately 70% of the quality of a professional. Most of the time that was enough. Plus, over time, I continued to improve my skills in many of those tasks and became as good as a professional specializing in those skills, or even better than them because my back was against the wall and I had to become great at some of the skills like marketing. If I didn't make myself great at marketing, business would not have survived.

This was a much slower way of doing things than giving a

task to a professional, and getting a polished result back quickly. But it was much cheaper in terms of spending cash. And now it is less time consuming because I don't have to ask anyone for help. Having acquired many skills needed by my business, I can just complete multiple tasks quickly and with a high degree of quality, and not have any delays in waiting for anyone.

This strategy isn't sustainable as a business grows and becomes bigger. But in the early stages of a business, I strongly recommend the approach that I described because it makes you a stronger entrepreneur, saves you money, and enables you to continue to push your business forward without depending on outside help.

iii. How to create a fundraising plan

A fundraising plan is a document that is internal to your business. It is a document on which you work with your team. It outlines how much money you will need, identify the resources and paths for where you can raise that money, and create a plan of action for actually raising the money you need to start your business.

Fundraising Plan Section: How Much Money Do You Need To Raise

Most people will take as much money as they can get. I would too. But that is not how you should approach writing this section of your fundraising plan. What you must do is identify the next important milestones your business needs to reach, and then calculate how much money you need in order to get to that milestone.

Imagine if you approach an investor, and the investor asks

you how much money you are looking to raise. If you say something like "as much as you can give me" that investor will not appreciate that answer no matter how true that answer actually is. What you should say is something like "I am looking to raise an X amount of money to get to the Y milestone. I will use that money to pay for A, B, and C." That is a much more professional answer.

Fundraising Plan Section: Fundraising Sources

In the next section we will go over the possible sources for raising money. Four of the fundraising sources are from institutions and the rest are things that depend on the entrepreneur's resourcefulness.

The Plan Of Action And Timeline

Try to outline how long each of your fundraising efforts is expected to take, and who on your team is responsible for carrying out those efforts.

The Risks

Once you have a sense for how long it will take you to raise the money to start your business from the different sources which you are planning to explore, consider whether the time and human effort which you plan to devote to your fundraising is worth the risk of possibly not raising that money, and whether it is worthwhile to go through with executing your fundraising plan in its current form.

iv. The 10 fundraising sources

Fundraising Source 1: Loans

Many entrepreneurs try to get small business loans to fund their businesses. The problem with getting a business loan is that by taking a loan to put towards your business, you risk money that you don't even have. That is double the risk of putting your savings into your business because if the business fails, you will still need to pay back that loan.

Most of the time, I try to talk people out of taking large business loans to start their businesses. Once the business has grown, loans are a very viable option to finance some of the operations of the business. But it is a very different situation if you have not started your business, and are looking to get a loan to actually start your business.

Despite my trying to talk people out of taking loans to start their businesses, people are adults, and ultimately make their own decisions. In this section of the book we will go over how to get a business loan, the difference between getting a personal loan and applying it to your business vs. getting an actual business loan, and a few other details. First, it is important to understand that banks do not make business loans to businesses which have not started.

Banks Do Not Make Business Loans To Companies Which Have Not Started

Many people who are looking to get a loan to help them start their business ask whether they can get a loan from a bank. Unfortunately, banks do not loan to businesses which have not started because loaning to businesses which have not started is too risky for a bank. Banks like predictability. And it is nearly impossible to determine how a business which has not started will do in the future. Small local banks may sometimes loan to a new business, but the majority of banks prefer to loan to established businesses which have regular revenue.

Usually large banks require two or more years of being in business and thousands of dollars in monthly revenue before they consider a company for a loan. Smaller, regional banks may have less of a requirement before they consider giving a business loan to a company, but they still require the business to be operational and to have revenue.

Possible Options Where You Can Get A Small Business Loan

There are two things you can do. You can take a personal loan, and spend that money on some of the things needed by your business. Or you can take a micro-loan.

There are a number of options for getting a micro-loan. Most micro-loans tend to be under $100,000. Some micro-loan companies are Kiva, Lendio, Prosper, and a few others. Each of these companies work in slightly different ways.

Lendio works by matching you with potential lenders according to your credit history, business type, location, and a number of other factors. To get matched with a lender, all a person has to do is fill out a form on Lendio. And if you are eligible for a loan, Lendio contacts you with further details and instructions for getting that loan from a lender with whom you are matched.

Prosper works by crowd-sourcing lending. For example, instead of finding a single lender who can lend thousands of dollars, Prosper can get many lenders to loan you the money by getting small amounts from many lenders.

Personal Loans vs. Business Loans

When people cannot get a business loan for their business, they can sometimes take out a personal loan and put that money towards starting their business. This is a possibility, but keep in mind that this increases your personal risk.

If you take out a business loan, and the business cannot pay it back, in most cases you are not personally liable for that loan. The business is liable. But if you take out a personal loan to apply to the business, you personally have to pay back that loan, and your credit history will suffer if you are not able to pay back that loan.

If you are getting a personal loan that you will want to put towards your business, your personal credit score will matter.

Pros And Cons Of Getting Business Loans

There are some strong opponents of getting business loans to fund your business. One of the loudest opponents of funding your business through loans is Marc Cuban who is an investor and entrepreneur. Marc's point is that since many businesses fail, most people will need to pay back the loan. So it is not any different than spending your own money. And people often take out much bigger loans than the amount they can realistically risk. That causes many people to lose money that they could not afford to lose. Marc is a big proponent of saving your money, paying back any outstanding loans you may have, and spending some of your savings to help you get your business started.

And of course, the advantage of being able to get a loan is that just like anything else, it is another weapon in your arsenal. And some of the time, it is the right tool. When people need a small amount of money that is perhaps under $20,000, if they can't easily get grants or investments to fund their business, getting a small loan can help them get started. So a small loan that they can get quickly might be the right option for them in that kind of a scenario. Of course they would need a way to pay that loan back, but nevertheless, having the option to be able to get a loan is a good option that may just be the right option in some cases.

Is It Possible To Get A Business Loan With Bad Credit?

If you have bad credit history, it is more difficult to get a business loan. If your business is already operational, and is doing well, the lender can look at the health of your overall business, and if the business is going well, that might compensate for your bad personal credit history. But until the business has built up its own credit history, you may have to personally underwrite your business loans.

NOTE: If you have bad credit, in most cases that refers to your personal credit history, and not the credit history/rating of the business. So the loan that you will need to get is a personal loan. That means you (and not the business) will need to pay it back. Be careful of secured loans. "Secured loans" means that the bank or whoever the lender is, can take away your possessions if you are not able to pay back the loan.

Fundraising Plan Source 2: Grants

Many entrepreneurs hope to get a grant to fund their small business, but the truth is that despite there being many grants out there, getting a grant is quite difficult. In fact, on my Problemio.com business apps, people ask precisely the question of how to get small business grants very often.

First of all, not everyone is even eligible for most grants. And even when people or businesses are eligible, they must search for grants that they can apply for, and compete with other organizations that are also trying to get that grant. The success rate of getting a grant to fund a small business is very low due to many takers. Additionally, nonprofit organizations are better candidates to get grants and government funding.

Grant Eligibility

If you are based in United States, to determine if you are eligible for a grant, visit the United States grant eligibility page or grants.gov. If you are not based in United States, just find the equivalent website for your country.

Grants are generally available to government organizations, educational organizations, public housing organizations, and nonprofits. Small for profit businesses and even individuals can also be eligible for grants, but that is less common.

Sources For Grants

When you research what grants you may be able to get, research whether there are any grants available to any local organizations or communities to which you may belong. If you are a part of a minority, there may be grants available to that minority. If you are a member of a religious group, there may be grants for members of that religious group. The same is true for any community you may belong to.

Additionally, cities and even particular neighborhoods try to stimulate local business growth by sometimes offering grants. Try to research whether those types of grants are available in your local area.

Fundraising Source 3: Investors

The next item to cover in your fundraising plan is whether you will be able to raise money from investors. Investors come in many different shapes and sizes and they tend to have very different methodologies and philosophies for how they like to invest. One good resource to find technology investors is AngelList.com and another is Gust.com.

The general overarching themes that investors do have are that they look for proven teams, high growth, and potential for large returns. Understanding that criteria, it is easy to deduce that most businesses do not fit that profile. Funding your company by getting an investment is almost always difficult. Nevertheless, here are some options and tips for funding your business by getting an investment.

Note, the below breakdown applies to investments in technology, and not businesses like common local services, restaurants, gyms, or other types of small businesses.

Investments From Friends And Family

You can get an investment from friends and family if your business is in a very early stage, or the business planning stage. Most professional investors might be hesitant to invest in a venture that is too new. So your friends and family might be a good source from which you may be able to raise an initial investment to get your business off the ground. Of course, many people do not like to get their friends and family involved in their business because they not want to risk the health of those relationships. Nevertheless, friends and family are the easiest source from which you can get an investment.

Seed Stage Investments

Seed stage investments are typically made by professional

investors. These investments can range from $50,000 - $750,000 depending on many factors. To get a seed stage investment, you typically need have already started your business, and be able to demonstrate some type of growth and product adoption in the marketplace.

Angel Stage Investments

This kind of investment can overlap with seed stage investments. The overlap is both in the types of investors who invest at this stage, and the amounts of money that is put in. Angel investments tend to be slightly bigger than seed state investments, and typically go to businesses which can demonstrate more market adoption than companies that get seed stage investments. The distinction between seed and angel investments is quite blurred.

Series A, B, And C Stage Investments

There is a lot of talk of raising venture capital, but the truth is that very few companies can ever even be considered for this type of an investment. Venture capitalists require steady and phenomenal growth, a gigantic market after which your company is going, and a slew of other factors. Most companies never qualify for venture money and that is not necessarily a bad thing. Raising venture capital can hurt the company because it limits the options you have as a company. The venture capitalists who invest want fast growth and to shoot big. That might sound nice, but their money often comes with many unneeded pressures that can do considerable damage to your company, and limit your strategy options.

Where You Can Go Wrong

Many people want to get an investment too early in the

development of their business. There are a few things wrong with that. First of all, the earlier you are, the least likely you will get your business funded. Most of the time when people try to get an investment for their company at a too-early stage, they just end up wasting their time which could be better spent on figuring out how to actually grow the company.

Another problem with seeking investment too early is that even in the unlikely event that an investment can be secured, the deal will probably favor the investor, and the entrepreneur will get very poor deal terms.

Additionally, be careful of bad investors, or taking money from someone who may not be a good fit for the kind of a company that you are trying to grow.

Fundraising Source 4: Donations

The next item to focus on in your fundraising plan is how you may be able to raise donations. Donations can be raised in a few ways. You can open an nonprofit for which you can raise donations using the old-fashioned way by mailing past customers, or calling them. If your nonprofit is a charity, you can raise money by seeking donations from wealthy individuals who use donations to get tax write-offs.

Another way to get donations is through a relatively new way to get donations, called crowdfunding. Crowdfunding takes advantage of the power of the Internet and allows many people to donate relatively small amounts to a project in which they believe. Together, those small amounts can add up to a large sum. That is great for the entrepreneur starting the project because it gives them some free money with nearly no strings attached.

Crowdfunding is only a few years old, but it is rapidly growing, and many projects have already raised tens of thousands and even millions of dollars via this method of funding.

Raising Donations Via Crowdfunding On Kickstarter

A site called kickstarter.com is the leader in this space. Originally they only allowed art projects to get funded, but now they are allowing a broader range of projects. Their rules do frequently change to accommodate their growth and the evolving laws around crowdfuning, so for current rules, and to see if you are eligible to apply, check their site.

Raising Donations Via Crowdfunding With IndieGogo

The second biggest crowdfunding site is indiegogo.com which is essentially a slightly smaller version of kickstarter. So if for some reason kickstarter does not work for you, you can possibly use indiegogo.

Raising Donations Via Crowdfunding With GoFundMe

GoFundMe.com isn't one of the leaders in this space, but it is one of the most flexible crowdfunding sites. There is no deadline for when your crowdfunding campaign should end like there is on Kickstarter, and any type of project can get funded on GoFundMe.

Specialized Crowdfunding Sites

There are many crowdfunding sites that specialize in funding various niches. For example, appstori.com specializes in crowdfunding for mobile apps. Science projects can get funding via petridish.org. There are many such sites popping up (and often closing down) since this is a very new space. So if you are interested in crowdfunding, search for the kind of crowdfunding site that may work best for your type of project.

Some crowdfunding sites are more effective than others at helping you raise money. You have to judge which crowdfunding site is right for you based on the nature of your project, and your funding needs. If you do want to give crowdfunding a try, you need to do understand how crowdfunding really works.

How CrowdFunding Really Works: The Inside Scoop

The way these sites grow is by having the entrepreneur in charge of the project which they hope to fund, invite friends to donate to the project and promote their crowdfunding campaign. The crowdfunding sites can help new people find your project, but most of the time the entrepreneur who is fundraising has to put in a big effort promoting their project, and try to find people to donate to the project. That means that you must do quite a bit of work in order to sufficiently promote your crowdfunding project.

Additionally, most crowdfunding sites take 4% of the total money raised.

Other Ways To Raise Money

The next fundraising sources depend more on your resourcefulness.

Fundraising Source 5: Get Part-Time Or Full-Time Work

Let's stop and consider what happens if you get a full time or part time job to fund your business. You will be able to save from a few hundred to a few thousand dollars a month. And you will also have a chance to learn about the industry in which you will do business if the job you get is in the same field as your business. That makes this a good option because you can get paid to learn the industry within which you will be starting your business. The challenge with this approach is that you can't raise too much money if your business needs hundreds of thousands of dollars.

Your humble author personally funded his Problemio.com mobile apps business by working and saving money to fund and bootstrap that business. That allowed me to not have to rely on outside sources like investors, and I was able to remain independent and focus on growing my business. So this is quite a good option to fund your business.

Fundraising Source 6: Get Money From The Revenue Of The Business

Being able to earn revenue with your business is a great way to fund your business. This approach to funding your company is actually the best long-term way to sustain your business. It will help you to not have to rely on investors or other kinds of institutions. Additionally, this is the most natural way for your business to raise money. Note that if you raise money from loans or investors, that process has nothing to do with running your actual business. But if you raise money through your own revenue, that effort has everything to do with getting your actual business to function right.

Fundraising Source 7: Creative Ways To Raise Money

Sometimes you can raise money by doing something creative. Here is one example. A few years ago I was trying to grow a group hiking site. It was difficult and I never raised money for it from investors, donations, or any other source like that. But I started doing cool hiking events like hikes to find lost shipwrecks or old cannons that were in the area. By having those intriguing hike themes, I was able to get many people to attend, some of whom I charged money for attending. That turned out to be great for my business because not only was I able to generate extra cash for the business, but I got exercise by going on the hikes, met many people, and the interesting hikes gave me an extra way to promote my website which resulted in many new website users. The money I raised this way helped me fund parts of that business. And the great thing about such events is that they can happen on a regular basis. So once you find something that works, you can do it over and over.

Fundraising Source 8: Get Money Upfront From Future Customers By Offering Them Discounts.

This is possibly one of the more savvy ways to raise money. Here is a case study from a business I am aware of that raised money this way. There was a company that was building a product for bars and pubs. But it didn't have the money to fully develop the product. So they went to a number of bars and talked to their owners. They convinced a number of the owners to put some money towards the development of the product in exchange for a deep discount in the future. And that allowed this new business to raise the money that they needed to develop their product, right from their future customers. They not only raised money, but also got customers at the same time, without even having a product!

Fundraising Source 9: Educational Classes And Workshops

Almost any business niche has some expertise to that can be shared with beginners in that niche. You can turn that expertise into online and offline educational resources. For example, you can hold workshops or classes for different things. And online you can create classes that can be sold on udemy.com or skillshare.com and earn passive income that way. You can also write books or make YouTube videos with similar educational material. All of these strategies will help you earn revenue that you can put towards your business. This strategy will also help you promote your business in addition to generating revenue.

Fundraising Source 10: Provide Services Online

Whatever your expertise may be, you can generate extra revenue by doing some work online. For example, there are many sites that help you earn money. Some of these are odesk.com, elance.com, fiverr.com, various other online concierge websites, sites like clarity.fm where technology experts help entrepreneurs, or any other service marketplace. You can use those sites to do work from home that will help you earn money which you can use in your business.

Part 7: FURTHER RESOURCES

If you have questions or comments about this book, please feel welcome to reach out to me. I would love to hear from you. Here is my personal email:
alex.genadinik@gmail.com

Additionally, here is my main website:
http://www.problemio.com

Here is my blog:
http://www.glowingstart.com

Here is my YouTube channel with over 500 business tutorials. I add new videos every day:
https://www.youtube.com/user/Okudjavavich

Here is a tutorial for how to set up your blog on your own in under one day:
http://www.problemio.com/website.html

Additionally, I also offer multiple online courses for starting and growing your business. Use discount code "nine" to get any of them for just $9. For some of the courses that is as much as a 90% discount.
https://www.udemy.com/u/alexgenadinik/

ABOUT THE AUTHOR

Alex Genadinik is a software engineer, an entrepreneur, and a marketer. Alex is the creator of the Problemio.com business apps which are some of the top mobile apps for planning and starting a business with 300,000 downloads across iOS, Android and Kindle. Alex has a B.S in Computer Science from San Jose State University.

Made in the USA
Middletown, DE
20 January 2018